Stop Domestic Violence

Stop Domestic Violence

An Action Plan for Saving Lives

Lou Brown
François Dubau
Merritt McKeon, J.D.

St. Martin's Griffin ❧ New York

Design by Maureen Troy

Library of Congress Cataloging-in-Publication Data

Brown, Louis (Louis Hezekiah)
    Stop domestic violence : an action plan for saving
lives / by Louis Brown, François Dubau, Merritt McKeon.
        p.   cm.
    Includes bibliographical references.
    ISBN 0-312-16611-7
    1. Family violence—United States.   2. Family violence—
United States—Prevention.   3. Wife abuse—United States—
Prevention.   I. Dubau, François.   II. McKeon, Merritt.
III. Title.
HQ809.3.U5B76   1997
362.82'92'0973—dc21   96-40417
                                                  CIP

First St. Martin's Griffin Edition: April 1997

10   9   8   7   6   5   4   3   2

*For Nicole and Ron
and the thousands of other
men, women, and children who are
victims of domestic violence and
whose stories are, all too often,
never told.*

Contents

part 1

Understanding Domestic Violence

part 2

Letters to the Battered Woman

Preface

We are very grateful that you are reading this book. We are honored to have worked on it. How often does a writer get to work on a book that is certain to save lives? This was the great motivation behind this project. The three of us come from completely different backgrounds, but we share one thought: most people do not understand domestic violence. We know that education on this issue will save lives.

We see this book as a new approach to the protection of women and children. Domestic violence is hidden, but it is everywhere and in every neighborhood. The more it is openly discussed, the less it will be able to remain concealed.

Lou Brown has come through his own set of extraordinary circumstances, and as a person who deals with these issues every day at the Nicole Brown Simpson Charitable Foundation and Legal Action Fund, he knows how important education can be. A gentle man determined that good will come out of his daughter's senseless suffering, he has been a quiet but powerful force in the development of this book.

Merritt McKeon is a survivor of domestic violence. After a stay in battered women's shelters, she went on to complete her bachelor's degree and then her master's. More recently she finished law school; she is currently a law professor. She plans to work as an attorney representing battered women, and she hopes to make legal representation more available to victims and survivors of domestic violence.

François Dubau is a pastor who was ordained by Chuck Smith, founder of Calvary Chapel, a nondenominational Protestant church. François started a ministry for the healing of the deepest emotional hurts in the lives of Christian men and women. This was in the midst of a great controversy about the use of psychology or therapeutic techniques in the church; many insisted that psychotherapy bordered on the heretical. What François saw proved to him that people were being healed in a new and profound way. He also saw the effects of domestic violence: how and where it begins in childhood, how it works in male and female adults, and how society in general avoids facing the problem.

Merritt and François have known each other since childhood; their friendship spans more than twenty-six years. Lou and Merritt have been talking and researching this book for a year and a half, and with François's enthusiastic "Let's pull this thing together" attitude, the book was researched, written, and double-checked. The final result, we hope, will be an important resource for ending family violence. It's tough enough to be in a really bad or violent relationship, but it's even harder to leave when those around the victim don't understand why it happened or what they can do to help.

This is the book Merritt wishes she'd had when she was trying to get out of her violent relationship. This is a book we hope will help build a network of support for those people who feel isolated.

Part One, "Understanding Domestic Violence," was written primarily by François. He combined his own counseling experience with the best literature and research available on domestic violence. Merritt wrote the last chapter of this section, "Who Speaks for the Kids?" which has footnotes so lawyers can use the information in helping battered women win their cases.

Part Two, "Letters to the Battered Woman," was written by Merritt. Her personal background has made her an undisputed expert. If you are a victim or survivor, you may want to start Part Two right away, to help build a plan of recovery.

Lou Brown wrote the Foreword—and he did so much more. The book grew out of many discussions that Merritt and Lou had long before the book's first words were written. When François and Merritt completed the manuscript, Lou read every word and made suggestions throughout. Without his inspiration and knowledge, this book would never have seen the light of day.

Stop Domestic Violence was also written with a great love and concern for victims and survivors, and for their friends and their families.

We encourage those of you who have been directly affected by this evil to turn it around: take the evil and the pain and turn them into good. This book will help you do that.

Please keep reading. Please go on to teach others what you're about to learn. Please be an activist, even if only to write a letter or raise funds. The Epilogue will tell you how.

Let's work together to end domestic violence. Reading this book will, we hope, be only the first step toward your becoming a light, an agent for change and recovery, in the shadowy world of family violence.

Lou Brown
François Dubau
Merritt McKeon

Foreword

I'll admit that when I first learned that my daughter Nicole was the victim of domestic violence, I cried.

I wept to think of my "little girl" cowering in terror as her husband raged. And even now I weep every time the television news catches me off guard by showing the photos of a bruised Nicole taken at the police station after she was battered.

I cannot tell you the rage and sadness I felt and still feel.

But my daughter was not the only battered woman in America. Far from it. According to the American Medical Association, husbands and boyfriends severely assault as many as 4 million women every year.

And, shockingly, one out of every four American women is likely to become a victim of domestic violence in her lifetime.

These are staggering statistics. But imagine them in real-life terms: imagine that one of every four of your women friends, relatives, and neighbors is potentially a victim.

For too long, women like my daughter—and your relatives, friends, and neighbors—have tried, and mostly failed, to handle violent, abusive spouses entirely on their own.

This is because for too long America's judicial system has failed these women. Police and courts often refuse to make arrests, giving perpetrators slap-on-the-wrist sentences, then releasing convicted abusers to go and harm their wives, girlfriends, and families once more.

It's time for this outrage to stop. It's time for decent Americans like us to band together and say, "No more" to these cowards who lift their hands in anger against their defenseless victims.

Please let me share with you some of what I have learned through hard personal experience—and what every caring American citizen needs to know.

You can help stop an American epidemic!

I know it's hard to understand how domestic violence happens in a family—and how it can keep happening over years and even decades. Until I learned about Nicole's situation, I didn't understand it myself.

But today, now that I know more, it hurts me deeply when I hear people say, "Well, it's her own fault if she stays with him. Any woman who would put up with that kind of treatment deserves what she gets!"

The fact is, women like my daughter stay with their abusive spouses for many reasons. And they want the father of their children to be part of the family.

Many battered women desperately want to believe their abusers' promises that it won't happen again. They are often made to feel worthless, because that's what the abusers tell them. And they are ashamed—deeply ashamed.

Sometimes a woman will stay with her abusive husband because she has no other place to go, or because he has threatened to kill her or her family or take the children if she leaves.

In fact, one of the most traumatic aspects of domestic violence is the *lifelong* effect on the lives of these children. Having learned life in a violent home, boys are inclined to follow the example set by a father; girls may follow their mother's submissiveness and never attain their full potential. The mind is scarred for life by the memory of violence.

And since former U.S. Surgeon General C. Everett Koop found that domestic violence is the number-one cause of injury among women in America, battered wives have every reason to take their husband's threats seriously.

Even more appalling, batterers become more violent when their wives are pregnant—and domestic violence is now the number-one cause of birth defects and miscarriages!

But despite all that we know about domestic violence, the courts and the police all too often handle batterers with kid gloves, showing more concern for preserving the criminal's rights than for showing compassion or administering justice to the victims!

The result? The assaults, rapes, and murders continue, despite all we have learned about domestic violence—despite our "enlightenment" about this horrendous problem.

Consider this one fact from the U.S. Department of Justice: in 29 percent of all violence against women by a lone offender, the perpetrator was an intimate (husband, ex-husband, boyfriend, ex-boyfriend).

That's almost one-third of all violent acts against women in the United States of America being committed by men who claim to love them.

I hope you have never experienced domestic violence, as a victim or as a victim's parent, sister, daughter, or friend.

Before I learned of Nicole's abuse, I never wanted to be in the limelight. I'm not a publicity-seeking man; I'm just an average husband and father trying to build a good life for my family.

But now that Nicole's tragedy has focused the public spotlight firmly on our family, I feel I am in an ideal position to help make a meaningful difference, to lead the charge against domestic violence on the national level. In fact, I believe that God is calling me to undertake this important work, and that we can create something positive out of our immeasurable loss.

That is why we took our first step in 1994: establishing the Nicole Brown Simpson Charitable Foundation.

But we couldn't stop there. Funding women's shelters is a little like putting a bandage on a cancer that is eating away at our society. The Band-Aid is urgently needed, but we must do more. We must cure this cancer—and that is why I established a second organization in 1996 that will work tirelessly to fully criminalize domestic abuse and punish offenders: the Nicole Brown Simpson Legislative Action Fund.

In setting up the fund, I thought about Mothers Against Drunk Driving (MADD). As you may remember, Candy Lightner, another parent who tragically lost a daughter, started MADD because she could no longer simply watch while people drove under the influence of alcohol and the police and courts did little or nothing to arrest, convict, and punish the offenders.

Through MADD's grassroots legislative action, the number of drunk driving deaths in the United States has declined dramatically.

We must do the same thing to stop the scourge of domestic violence.

Our first priority is to rally massive grassroots public support for the passage of important legislation and pass laws that will *force the courts to treat and punish abusive husbands and boyfriends as the criminals they really are,* laws that will *protect the rights of domestic violence victims.*

The death penalty should be considered in sentencing domestic violence offenders who kill their spouses or partners.

Evidence concerning the abuser's prior treatment of the victim must be admitted into court in criminal cases.

Medical evidence—the battered-woman's syndrome—must be admitted into the proceedings in domestic violence cases. This is particularly crucial in addressing why an abused woman might have stayed with her husband or delayed reporting the crime.

Domestic violence offenders must be required to take a test for HIV—the virus that causes AIDS—before the trial and at specified intervals after conviction. Results of the HIV test would then be reported to the victim. This provision is absolutely crucial in protecting the victim's health and the health of her children.

It is time for all of us, as individuals and as a society, to stop looking the other way. It is time we all helped put a stop to this plague of vicious brutality.

I ask your pledge and dedication to this cause.

LOU BROWN
The Nicole Brown Simpson Charitable Foundation
15 Monarch Bay Plaza
Box 380
Monarch Beach, CA 92629

Part 1

Understanding Domestic Violence

Chapter 1

What Is Domestic Violence?

There is a secret war in America, and in it millions of our citizens are held hostage, beaten, threatened, and killed. A recently released U.S. Department of Justice report, based on the National Crime Victimization Survey (NCVS), confirms the national problem of violence against women:

- *In 1992 and 1993, almost 5 million violent crimes were committed annually against women age twelve or older.*

- *Nearly 75 percent of all lone-offender violence against women was perpetrated by someone whom the victim knew.*

- *In 29 percent of all violence against women by a lone of-fender, the perpetrator was an intimate—a husband, ex-husband, boyfriend, or ex-boyfriend.*

- *Women annually reported 500,000 rapes and sexual assaults, almost 500,000 robberies, and about 3.8 million assaults.*

- *An estimated 1,432 women were killed by domestic violence in 1992.*

While we are learning more about it every day, one thing is clear to everyone: when dealing with any aspect of domestic violence, the first thing we are all going to need is *patience.*

Patience is something most people don't have much of when they first try to help someone trapped in domestic violence. Consider these words from Robin Yeamans, an attorney who has twenty-five years of experience representing battered women in California:

> *What I've learned over the years is to try to go at a pace that is acceptable to the battered woman, though it may seem incredibly slow to me. Some lawyers become outraged and rush to court, get restraining orders immediately, and then the woman backs off. I try to wait until the woman is firmed up enough that she'll be able to hang in there through the legal process. It's like a dance, and I can't dance fast with her if she wants to dance slow.*
>
> *The other thing I've learned is not to be discouraged, or surprised, when these women reconcile [with their batterers]. I just assure them that if they want help in the future, I'll be there.*

Patience is needed all around. Our society is just now awakening to the violence being done to women.

To present to you the most accurate information and statistics regarding domestic violence in America, we chose the most widely respected source: the U.S. Department of Justice and its Bureau of Justice Statistics. Here is what the Bureau itself says of its statistics: "Estimating rates of violence against women, particularly sexual assault and other incidents which are perpetrated by intimate offenders, continues to be a difficult task. Many factors inhibit women from reporting these victimizations both to police and to interviewers, including the private nature of the event, the perceived stigma associated with one's victimization, and the belief that no purpose will be served in reporting it."

One of the latest reports from the Department of Justice on violence against women, completed in August 1995, contained the following points:

1. *Women age twelve or older annually sustained almost 5 million violent victimizations in 1992 and 1993.*

2. *About three-quarters of all lone-offender violence against women and 45 percent of violence involving multiple offenders were perpetrated by offenders whom the victim knew.*

3. *In 29 percent of all violence against women by a lone offender, the perpetrator was an intimate (husband, ex-husband, boyfriend, or ex-boyfriend).*

4. *Women were about six times more likely than men to experience violence committed by an intimate.*

5. *Women annually reported to interviewers about 500,000 rapes and sexual assaults. Friends or acquaintances of the victims committed over half of these rapes or sexual assaults. Strangers were responsible for about 1 in 5.*

6. *Among victims of violence committed by an intimate, the victimization rate of women separated from their husbands was about three times higher than that of divorced women and about twenty-five times higher than that of married women. Because the NCVS reflects a respondent's marital status at the time of the interview, which is up to six months after the incident, it is possible that separation or divorce followed the violence.*

7. *Female victims of violence by an intimate were more often injured by the violence than females victimized by a stranger.*

Violence against women perpetrated by people they knew intimately was consistent across racial and ethnic boundaries. No statistically significant difference existed between groups.

In the first few weeks after murder charges were filed against O. J. Simpson, and the world learned about his abuse of Nicole, the media suddenly discovered domestic violence. Suddenly, also, all the battered women's shelters, hotlines, and coalition groups found themselves overwhelmed with phone calls from victims desperately seeking help for the first time. All of us in America have been touched by Nicole's tragedy.

This book is a guide to saving lives. Read and share with others what you learn; you will begin to help battered women, simply by knowing how to help them. You will understand the problem, and this will go far helping to end it. The city of San Diego, California, has a program that provides this information to high school students, college students, police, attorneys, judges, and anyone else who will listen. The city's homicide rate in domestic violence cases has dropped 60 percent. *Education saves lives.*

How many female victims of domestic violence were victimized repeatedly? About one in five women victimized by a spouse or ex-spouse reported to the NCVS that in the last six months they had experienced three or more assaults so similar that the victim could not distinguish one from another. For assaults in general in 1992, fewer than one in ten crimes involved this type of victimization.

During the past five years, rates of rapes, robberies, and assaults committed by intimates on both male and female victims have been constant. According to the NCVS, between 1987 and 1992, the rate of violent victimizations committed by intimates varied little from the average annual rate of 5 per 1,000 for females and 0.5 per 1,000 for males. The proportion of all violence that was committed by intimates also stayed consistent, at about 27 percent of all violence against females and about 2 percent of all violence against males.

According to the NCVS, 18 percent of women raped, robbed, or assaulted by intimates faced an armed offender, compared to 33 percent of those victimized by strangers, 22 percent of those targeted by other relatives, and 21 percent of those victimized by acquaintances. When the assailant was an intimate and weapons were present, 40 percent of crimes involved knives or sharp instruments, 34 percent involved guns, 12 percent involved blunt objects, and 15 percent involved other weapons. Strangers, compared with other types of offenders, were more likely to be armed with guns.

Do you want to do something about domestic violence? Keep reading. This is the most vital first step: learning about and discussing with others the topic of domestic violence.

It takes courage to read a book of this kind. If a woman you know has given you this book to read, ask yourself some questions: Why has she given you this book? Who are you in her life? Is she reaching out to you because she needs help? Does she simply want to talk about this issue with you? Is she in a relationship right now that endangers her? Perhaps she's been hiding the battering and now is reaching out to you for help through this book. Do you have a mutual friend or relative? Perhaps she is giving you this book to read because she wants to enlist your help for that friend. Are you a man with an abusive temper? Perhaps your friend hopes you can learn something about this problem before it ruins your life and destroys your family. Before you come to any conclusions, read this book. Then ask her why she's given it to you.

Even if she is a victim, she may not want your help right now. When women are victimized by people they know, 18 percent *do not report* the violent victimization to police because they are afraid of worse violence from the abuser. (In contrast, only one-sixth as many women victimized by strangers fail to report the crime for this reason.) This raises the question: *How many women do we know right now who are keeping domestic violence a secret?*

Families and friends of victims of domestic violence often wonder what they can do to help the person they love. The more we know about domestic violence, the more we can understand the pain and isolation of the victim.

First, understand that although you may find it hard to believe that the husband or boyfriend is really being violent, most batterers have a "public face" and show their violent "private face" only to the victim, when she is trapped and there are no witnesses.

Second, when you begin to interact with a battered woman the first thing you need to do is *listen to her.* Listen to her without telling her what she should or shouldn't do. Just let her speak. Let her get it all out in the open. Ask only small questions to clarify what she is saying. Do not interrupt the flow of her thoughts as she is telling you what's happened to her. Be there, and be as quiet as possible. There is a great healing value in listening. You will do your friend a great service by keeping quiet. If you are in doubt as to whether you should ask her a question or not, it's usually better not to ask, just to let her talk.

Another vitally important thing is to let her know that *she is not at fault.* The fault is with the batterer, not with her. If she has a drug or alcohol addiction, or if he does, she can and must seek help in a Twelve Step program such as Alcoholics Anonymous or Al-Anon (a support program for people involved with an alcoholic or addict). Of course, not all alcoholics or drug abusers are batterers, and not all batterers are drug or alcohol abusers, so AA and Al-Anon won't be for everyone. And information about them must be shared lovingly and without judgment, because even the best advice can sound like "You, the victim, are to blame" to someone in the early stages of seeking help.

Two things we must do to stop domestic violence in America:

First, learn about domestic violence and discuss it with others.

Second, if a battered woman tells you about her situation, the first thing to do is listen to her. She may have a pretty good idea of what help she needs, and you may be able to assist her get that help. Also, she really needs people who understand and a society that won't allow the violence to continue. That's where the first step will help stop this terrible problem.

How do we define domestic violence?

Domestic violence is a criminal act of assault, battery, sexual assault, sexual battery, or other act that injures or kills a family or household member by another who is or was residing in the same single dwelling unit.

Physical or verbal abuse doesn't take place in a vacuum. A battered spouse may be controlled and terrorized by a combination of abusive tactics, not always physical acts. There is a pattern in the relationship: one of the people is the victim. *In over 90 percent of cases of domestic violence recorded by the NCVS from 1987 to 1991, the victim was female.*

Some things statistics cannot identify; other things are blunt, brutal, and obvious. We do know that:

- Women are not battering their husbands in epidemic proportions.

- Women are not regularly beating up their men and leaving them crouched, huddled, sobbing, and injured (or worse) on the kitchen floor.

- Men are not fleeing their homes, children in tow.

- Men are not the spouses who live in terror.

Let's enter the world of battered women. What you are about to read includes graphic language, which is necessary to make the point:

"Who is that [on the phone]!" he demands.

She ignores him, hastily whispering, "I gotta go now. . . ."

"*Gimme* that phone!" he shouts. "Who was that!"

"It was someone from work."

He dials call return. It wasn't someone from work. "You sniveling, lying *bitch!*" he shrieks—and, yanking the phone out, throws it into the wall. "*You tell me who the f—— that was right now!*" He advances on her, then picks up a little glass bud vase her grandmother gave her and holds it high.

"No, gimme that!" she cries.

"Who the f—— was on that phone?"

She grabs his arm to save the vase, and he holds it out of her reach. Then: *SMASH!* The vase shatters into a thousand shards.

"You pig," she mutters, nearly inaudible.

"What'd you say? Say it again, bitch!" he screams. She crouches on the floor, attempting to scoop up glass splinters. He grabs her by the upper arm, bringing her to her feet. She wrenches her arm away; as he reaches for her again, she pushes his forearm away from her.

"I wanna know who was on that phone!" he yells down, close into her face, as she backs away.

"No one . . ."

"You stupid lying cow!" he shouts, and shoves her hard enough to fling her into the corner of the wall, where she hits her head.

There are six kinds of abuse by which batterers exercise power and control over their victims. They are these:

• **PSYCHOLOGICAL ABUSE:** The batterer tries to frighten the victim by intimidating her, threatening to harm her or others, threatening to kidnap her, harassing her, or killing pets and destroying property.

• **EMOTIONAL ABUSE:** The batterer undermines his victim's sense of self-worth by constant criticism, belittling, name calling, the silent treatment, subverting parent-child relationships, making and breaking of promises, and so forth.

• **ECONOMIC ABUSE:** This includes making, or trying to make, a person financially dependent—for instance, by maintaining control over both parties' income, withholding money or access to money, keeping the victim from outside activities such as school or employment, harassing the victim at work, and requiring her to justify all money spent.

• **SEXUAL ABUSE:** Sexual abuse is coerced (unconsenting) sexual contact—for instance, rape and beating of the sexual parts of the body, as well as forced bestiality, prostitution, unprotected sex, fondling, sodomy, sex with others, or use of pornography. Sexual abuse may also include undermining a person's sexuality with insults and unfounded accusations of infidelity. Rape in marriage is illegal, yet it happens all too often. Rape can happen if intercourse starts while the victim is asleep.

• **PHYSICAL ABUSE:** This is hurting someone or trying to hurt her—for instance, by grabbing, pinching, shoving, slapping, hitting, hair pulling, biting, arm twisting, kicking, punching, hitting with objects, stabbing, shooting. Other kinds of physical abuse include withholding access to resources necessary to maintain health: e.g., medications, medical care, a wheelchair, food or fluids, sleep, hygienic assistance. An abuser may also force his victim to use alcohol or drugs.

• **LEGAL ABUSE:** The abuser may drag his victim through a vicious custody battle or an expensive court case when she leaves him. He may give her less than she deserves by law and may drag out the proceedings. He may refuse to pay court-ordered support or alimony or to turn over assets. This may sound like a typical divorce, but abusive divorces continue a pattern of abuse established in the marriage. Incredibly, the abuser often tries to win back his spouse during or after the abusive divorce. More incredibly yet, she sometimes goes back to him. (This is a part of the cycle of violence, which we will learn about in the next chapter.) The point is, the abuse does not end when the woman leaves. It can continue in another form.

General Facts About Domestic Violence

Abuse is about power and control. It often starts out with non-violent forms of control, then escalates, when the abuser still does not feel "enough" in control (of the woman or his life or both), to physical violence. But even before that point, the relationship's power dynamics are not equal. Regardless of who first did what to whom physically, only one of the parties is the victim. Because he is rewarded (by "winning"), over time the abuser escalates the methods he uses to exert control. Before any physical violence is ever employed, the power imbalance and control are established. The situation "creeps up" on the woman, so she simply doesn't see how she is coming under tighter and tighter controls and more and more abuse.

This is the point where common sense breaks down. Most people who have never been abused this way can't understand why the victim doesn't see what's happening to her and doesn't just leave. Ignorance regarding this specific point is massive. We need to put away all gut-level reactions and think the matter through. This is a critical point; close attention is needed if we are to understand the dynamics involved.

Our concept of "normal" and the domestic violence victim's concept of "normal" are completely different. Don't try to force your concept of "normal" upon a victim of domestic violence. If you do, you may frighten her away from reaching out to anyone else and push her back further into her ordeal. Instead, listen to her uncritically and without offering your opinion; as you do this enough times, she will regain her senses. Do, however, encourage her to pick up this book herself. Part Two may be a first step to getting her to plan her way "out."

Unfortunately, "normal" for the victim becomes the periods between episodes of physical abuse. But the situation is never normal. If he hits her once, he *will* do it again. And he'll do worse.

You are facing a situation where, on the one hand, the woman needs to get out but must do so on her own schedule, while on the other hand, if she stays she may be battered again. Yet *this is standard in domestic violence.* The situation is often crazy, but don't give up on your friend. Be patient and recognize that this person's life is in serious danger. She is a prisoner and you're helping her plan her escape.

Battered women do not start out as "wimps." This is a myth that we all need to abandon. Another myth is that batterers are wild-eyed Hell's Angels types, chasing women down the street with a crowbar. These are comic-book images. Real batterers come in all shapes, incomes, sizes, and backgrounds. One cop friend told us recently that after going on domestic violence calls for years he could describe the typical batterer in his precinct this way: he wears a suit and tie, earns a six-figure income, drives an imported car, and projects an image of perfect respectability. If the victim calls the police, she spends the weekend at an expensive hotel to get better. This cop's precinct is an up-and-coming suburb of Los Angeles.

It's even more surprising to meet an extremely successful woman who is highly motivated, financially independent, an expert in her field, and completely together on the outside, but has become the victim of a batterer. It may have started out as the best relationship on earth, one that was too good to be true. He was charming, boyish, vulnerable, eager, smooth, clever, and sexy; she fell in love quickly. The beginning of an abusive relationship often seems, when you look back, to have gone a little too fast, though at the time it just seemed perfect.

Before he discovered the guaranteed success of the iron fist, there may have been a control struggle in the relationship. The woman may have used passive-aggressive tactics, or even some physical aggression, in an effort to regain a measure of control over her own life. But when the man felt his control of her (or other things in his life) slipping away, he switched to a more potent "weapon." So it's not that victims are wimps to begin with, but that a batterer is typically a man with a twisted mind and a sophisticated ability to deceive, seduce, and brainwash his victim. The next chapter will explore the seductive nature of a batterer.

What's the Good News?

Nicole Brown Simpson's tragic death has had a most profound impact. Never before have so many Americans wanted to do something to help victims of domestic violence. Never before have so many batterers both felt pressure to stop and also known there was help available for them.

You, the person reading this book, are a powerful agent for change in the deliverance of women being beaten senselessly, the deliverance of children being subjected to this violence, and even the deliverance of batterers from themselves. Read, educate, practice patience, and stimulate conversation on domestic violence. We can all do at least this much. And this much is a lot: it is the foundation for a grassroots transformation of the consciousness of America on domestic violence.

If you want to do more, call your local shelters for battered women and ask what you can do. They need all kinds of support, from cans of food to people willing to raise money. Get a friend to help you. It's usually more fun to do volunteer work together. If there is no shelter in your community, start talking to people to get one started. Sometimes all it takes is one person talking to others; everyone suddenly feels the need to organize, and momentum builds. That's how shelters happen.

Finally, if this book has been given to you by a woman who is being battered and this is her way of reaching out to you for help, remember the first rule: listen to her. Listen to her as you've never listened to anyone before in your life. *The single best thing you can do for a battered woman when she first comes to you is to be quiet and just listen to her.*

Our greatest tool in the healing of this nation from this epidemic may be something we can all do equally well because it is so simple: listening to the person telling us her pain.

Chapter 2 - - - - - - - - - - - - - - - -

What Makes These Men Do It?

The questions on everyone's mind are these: Why don't abusive men stop, take a time-out, walk away—do *something*—when they start to feel violence coming up inside them? Why don't they go to therapy after the first episode and put a stop to their violence right away? Who can imagine someone like O. J. Simpson, a national sports hero, movie star, and successful businessman—in short, a man with everything any man could possibly want—turning out to have a Jekyll-and-Hyde personality, hurting his own wife?

When you start trying to figure out what makes these men tick, you enter a realm so foreign to normal experience that it astonishes you. You find men who are good-looking, intelligent, and successful, who have everything going for them, and you discover that they have another personality so completely different that *you can't believe it at first*. Abusive men are masters at projecting a public face characterized by charm, warmth, caring, and tenderness. Behind this public mask hides a raging batterer.

One reason why we have such a difficult time understanding men who beat and sometimes kill their wives or girlfriends—or their children—is that they violate our sense of normal decency. They do things that normal people would never do.

A second reason for our difficulty is that these men do things completely contrary to their own self-interest. Who in his right mind threatens, beats, even kills the person he loves most? How can abusers do such horrible things to their wives and children? It doesn't make any sense. Because it doesn't make any sense, the average person can't believe that someone he or she knows would do this.

A third reason is the social stigma associated with battering. Who can possibly accept being like this? Who can live with having to hide this kind of shameful behavior? Our common sense tells us that if we found this kind of horrible behavior starting to develop within ourselves, we would immediately seek help. We would go to a therapist, a psychiatrist, a mental health service, a priest, minister, or rabbi—maybe an exorcist! How can these men see this behavior take them over, yet not act against it once they have calmed down? Even if they are afraid of being in therapy, wouldn't they go for the ones they say they love? It doesn't seem reasonable that someone would do violence to his family and not immediately act to stop it. It's not in that man's best interest, and people tend to do what's in their best interest. After all, we are basically selfish!

Here are just three simple and commonsense reasons why domestic violence has been able to sink deep into the marrow of our culture. People don't want to believe that other human beings would do this. People don't want to associate with people who do this. People don't even want to talk about the subject. You can bet that with this resistance and denial at work throughout our culture, we have created a perfect climate for the worst kind of domestic violence to quietly grow and spread like a terrible disease.

Besides, there is a realm of reasons that defy common sense; the world of domestic violence resembles fantasy or science fiction. Once you start reading about and walking vicariously into the lives of battered women and batterers, you enter into a kind of twilight zone. In this environment, the air is poisoned with lies. This is not a place where normal human life can exist. Both the victims and the batterers are infected with toxic levels of deception. They lie to themselves about the fact that they lie; they think they're telling the truth. Lies are constantly wrapping themselves around lies as those involved try to convince everyone that they're telling the truth. Domestic violence is like a maze of mirrors; when you think you see the way out, you bump into your own reflection.

In this land, where lies are everywhere, the batterer begins to look like a victim, and the victim begins to look like a batterer. You encounter men who beat the life out of their women physically and emotionally, yet feel no remorse at all: their conscience was amputated long ago. You meet intelligent and capable women who are reduced to brainwashed, zombielike, faded copies of themselves. You start wondering whether you've left enough bread crumbs on the path so that you can find your way back to sanity and real life. You see a victim explaining that it is her fault; you see a batterer sending roses to the woman he put in the hospital. You begin to get a sense of what Alice must have felt when she entered Wonderland.

Yet these people are all around us. They look—and in many ways often are—normal, functional, reliable, successful people.

It does take courage to enter the world of domestic violence. The therapists, social workers, and others who work with batterers and victims are quiet and unsung heroes. They are on the front line, trying to reverse centuries of this creeping invasion of violence dedicated to the destruction of women and children. They are underpaid, overworked, and underappreciated. They need our help. Learning about the problem and teaching each other about the solutions is the first, all-important step toward ending domestic violence in America.

Once you have accepted the fact that the world of domestic violence is both alien and all around us, a question often comes up:

Are batterers victims or perpetrators, fallen angels or demons? Experts answer that they are both. Our common sense replies: How can they be both? It's either one or the other.

Donald G. Dutton and Susan Golant have written *The Batterer: A Psychological Profile,* an excellent book to help us understand the world of the batterer and answer the question that gives this chapter its title. Dutton gave expert testimony about wife assault for the prosecution in the O. J. Simpson murder trial. In *The Batterer,* he writes:

> *It's easy, given the atrocities against battered wives, simply to dismiss abusers as less than human or to see all men as inherently violent. . . . But if we do that, we draw a firm battle line between male and female, viewing all females as victims of intimate abuse and all males as the perpetrators. And drawing those lines limits our ability to understand.*
>
> *To perceive the male as both a victim and a perpetrator confuses this compartmentalized view, and yet I believe that this more complex perspective reflects the reality of abusiveness. There is evidence that abusive men . . . were once victims. . . . Their victimization does not excuse their behavior, but it does explain it.*

First, the batterer beats up on women to make himself feel like a whole person. The psychological explanation is that his own father's "shaming and violent behavior" and his mother's detachment and emotional unavailability have produced his violence. For such a man, women become lightning rods that attract and catch all his emotional damage. When he gets close to a woman emotionally, a sequence of reactions is triggered, and he ends up in a blind rage and beats up his victim.

Second, experts describe the abuse as happening in a pattern, a cycle: a buildup of tension is followed by a blowout, with full violence against the woman. This is made worse if the woman leaves him or becomes pregnant. In either situation, he will no longer have her completely to himself. If she goes to a shelter, he's lost her and he goes crazy. If she is pregnant, the baby will need her attention and she will have someone else in her life: he goes crazy.

However, if she does not protect herself by leaving after the blowout of violence, they enter the cycle's next phase, called the honeymoon. During the honeymoon, he lures her into having sex with him again, almost as if he must seal her back into the relationship. He does this to be certain she is still "his," much as an animal will mark its territory. This is terrible for the victim, since she is very vulnerable after she has been beaten. Just at her low point, he brings her back to him and she is once more in the relationship, confused again. *He* controls the cycle. She remains his victim until she learns to break free.

It's important to note that in these relationships a woman is often between a rock and a hard place. If, when he is saying crazy things to her, she tries to respond, to tell her side of the story, the batterer just gets angrier with every word she speaks. But if she says nothing, he feels that she is not giving him her full attention, and he goes wild. So she's damned if she answers him and damned if she says nothing. Also, as her self-esteem is destroyed by him, he builds it up by telling her she is the only woman he loves. A victim's self-esteem is always low: whether or not it was healthy to begin with, it will be low after a few rides on the violence cycle.

We must also realize that while abusive men were probably victims of their childhood, this cannot excuse the damage they do, as adults, to their spouses and children. After all, many boys who grow up in abusive homes become wonderful people, outstanding members of society. On the other hand, some people who come from happy families end up hateful and mean. But though batterers can't be excused, they do need help to heal themselves. You can and should lead these horses to water; the hard part is that you sure can't force them to drink.

We have to have compassion for the monster, while not being fooled by the former victim. This is not going to be easy.

Although many batterers have a history of being abused in childhood, all batterers are not alike. Each man has to be treated as an individual. He must be watched the way you would watch any potential source of danger. Without being deceived by the lies coming from this man, we need to hold on to the hope that he can be healed of this destructive behavior. Writing abusers off is not intelligent, loving, or healthy for ourselves and our society.

Dutton and Golant describe three broad categories of batterers: the psychopathic wife assaulters; the overcontrolled wife assaulters; and the cyclical/emotionally volatile wife abusers.

The psychopathic abuser is the man who seems to be missing a conscience. He feels no guilt after he's done something horrible to his spouse or girlfriend. The woman can end up in an intensive care unit at the hospital, yet the abuser's heart never skips a beat. Magnetic resonance imaging (MRI) studies of the brains of these men seem to indicate that their brains do not function like those of normal people. When psychopaths are observing emotionally provocative events, their MRIs look as though nothing is happening, while scans of the normal men's brains show huge color patterns radiating from the brain stem forward toward the temporal lobes. Psychopaths seem completely unable to imagine how what they are doing hurts the victim, or even to imagine the consequences to themselves. Other studies have even shown that these men become calmer and calmer inside as they assault their victim. About 20 percent of batterers fall into this subgroup; known as "vagal reactors," they become almost calm in the vortex of violence.

They respond like super-athletes who have achieved such mastery over their bodies that they can control their heartbeat, calming and focusing themselves, as they batter their victim. Here is something good twisted into something bad.

About 30 percent of batterers belong to the group of "overcontrolled wife assaulters." These men seem out of touch with their feelings and would rather be by themselves, but can erupt aggressively quite suddenly. They may be calm and under control for long periods; then, suddenly, some problem in their lives will trigger rage. These batterers are the most explosive and the ones who tend to get the press coverage. Within this category are two kinds of men: an active type, commonly known as a "control freak," and a loner who seems passive until he explodes. These loners are men big on what the "woman's role" is to be. They abuse women verbally, both when they're alone with them and in front of others. They show little affection at any time in the relationship.

Finally, the third group includes the cyclical/emotionally volatile abusers. Their wives describe them as having dual personalities: the classic Dr. Jekyll and Mr. Hyde, two completely different people in one body. Their buddies will say, "He's just one of the boys." Their wives will say, "I never know which one is coming through the door at night." These men are living contradictions: they're afraid of intimacy but are always involved with a woman. According to Dutton and Golant, these men "need to shame and humiliate another human being to finally obliterate their own shame and humiliation."

What makes these men—who make up about half of all abusers—act like this? How can they be one person one instant and a completely different person the next? Don't they see the evil side when it is battering their spouse or girlfriend? What causes them to lash out at one moment and become contrite and sorry the next? Why do they act this way only with their wife or girlfriend? Why only in private? Why do they experience such extreme fits of jealousy and rage?

And, after these men have committed violence against the person they love, how do they explain what they did?

There is a whole range of responses, from a total denial that anything happened, to attempts to make it up, to promises that he will change. Typically, a man will reconstruct the history of the event and completely blame the victim, saying that she started the whole thing and "made him" do it. But the opposite is also possible: the batterer may act deeply sorry for what he did, turn into a little kid, ask to be forgiven, and swear that he will never do it again. When you see what he's done to the woman and how he acts afterward, it is clear that he is partially insane.

What causes these men's behavior? Can they be treated and cured? Here, also, the situation is slightly maddening. It is not enough that the problem itself is difficult to understand, but the explanations and solutions offered by experts are equally complex, mutually contradictory, and altogether unconvincing.

In *The Batterer,* Dutton and Golant review the various schools of thought. There is a brain-damage theory, which holds that an "interruption to the oxygen supply during the birth or infancy or other traumatic scars" can explain the behavior of the adult batterer. There is the sociobiological view, also known as the genetic mandate theory, according to which the genetic makeup of these men is programmed with this type of violence as a result of the evolutionary development of the human race. Feminists argue that men have been abusing women since the Stone Age. They blame the Old Testament for advocating the stoning of women for committing adultery. They blame Christianity, which during the Inquisition and the witch trials in Europe saw 300,000 women burned at the stake. The feminist view "focuses on society rather than the individual as the cause of male abusiveness . . . and distrusts psychological causes [or explanations] of male violence," but here we disagree. Feminists generally say they want to see abusers take responsibility for their abuse and are angry that society and the legal system, from the police to the judges in our highest courts, don't establish that men who hit women will spend time in jail. (Merritt calls this the "Well, *duh* theory" of domestic violence: "If you can get away with something and don't see what's wrong with it, well, *duh*, you'll keep doing it.") Psychologists respond by saying that many or most men who grow up in the same culture are not abusive.

Social learning theory emphasizes "how habitual actions, such as violence, are acquired through observations of others, and how they are maintained by social payoffs called rewards." Batterers, according to this theory, are just copying what they saw around the house when they were growing up. Dutton concludes: "None of these theories answered all my questions about cyclical abusers, and some raised new ones."

Which school of thought best explains who batterers are, what they do, and whether they can be treated and healed? We can study how long the experts have been around, how long their theories have been around, what kind of programs they have engendered; we can examine their success rates. Who has treated how many men, and what percentage of those men have been successfully restored to a more normal life? Unfortunately, it's too early to evaluate the theorists' results. Because domestic violence has been denied or conveniently overlooked throughout the history of our culture, all the current approaches are relatively new. We need a few more decades to single out the best approach to treating and healing abusers.

In *The Batterer*, Donald Dutton presents his own explanation and describes the kind of therapy he has used to heal batterers. He has studied more than 700 men and has led therapy groups with hundreds more.

After all these years of work, what is the conclusion of this famous expert? Dutton writes:

> *Although my findings indicate the necessity and efficacy of treatment, we still have to be cautious in our interpretation. . . . No psychological treatment works for someone who has no motivation. No forced remedy has a lasting therapeutic effect, including brainwashing, electroshock, and castration. . . . After sixteen years of doing this work, I still find myself surprised. I have learned to be humbled in my power of prediction. There are men who I thought would never be able to stop beating their wives, but they have, for reasons that only partially have to do with therapy. . . . Every group has in it at least one man who seems hopeless but improves dramatically. That's what keeps me coming back for more.*

But if we don't know that abuse is taking place, and we don't help the victim in her search for sanity and safety, how can we "force" the batterer to get help? The solution, according to Merritt's *"duh* theory," is that we learn about domestic violence, recognize it when it happens, and help the victim find a safe way out of the relationship. Then the abuser can either be put in jail, be ordered into therapy, or be forced to move on to another relationship. We can only hope that women will learn to recognize the beginnings of abuse and will avoid abusive men. If enough of us learn to deal with violence on a one-to-one basis, eventually there will be lots of extremely lonely batterers who will seek therapy so they can get what they really need: a healthy relationship in their lives. Until that day, we must learn to protect the victim.

Chapter 3

Why Do Women Stay?

Common sense tells me that if I am in a situation that is painful, I leave. Common sense tells me that if a person doesn't leave, it's because she likes where she is. Common sense is completely off the mark in the case of domestic violence. We have seen how people who have not experienced domestic violence are often completely clueless about its dynamics. Sad to say, even when we're clueless on a particular subject, we often have an opinion about it anyway—even if that opinion is completely wrong. Let us debunk some "commonsense myths" about domestic violence.

First, women who are battered do not stay in these relationships because they like it. All studies in which battered women were asked if they liked being abused got a negative response. The idea that women do like abuse, which lurks in the back of many people's minds, is just not true.

Why, then, do women stay in these relationships, when they are beaten up, tortured, degraded, brainwashed, even killed? What could possibly keep them in these relationships?

There is an answer, but understanding it will take a little time; you may have to reread this chapter. Please give yourself and the subject some of that old magical cure for domestic violence: patience. And do not be surprised if the answer is not easy to accept. If you haven't experienced domestic violence, it will be difficult to understand some of what is said here. Nonetheless, we believe a satisfactory answer is now within our grasp.

A second myth we can dismiss immediately is that women caught in domestic abuse are always weak, physically, emotionally, financially, socially, or even spiritually. It's true that the victim will need to strengthen herself so that she can get out of the relationship: domestic violence will weaken or even destroy a woman. But we have seen time and time again that domestic violence can happen to anyone. Women who are physically strong, emotionally together, financially successful, socially accepted, and even spiritually ahead of most other women fall into the trap of domestic violence just as less healthy women do. Domestic violence is not a matter of her being weak. It is the nature of the crime that domestic violence weakens a woman on all levels, starting with her mind and spirit, moving on to her body, self-esteem, career, and finances; if she does not leave, it will take her life.

Why do women stay? That question is based on a third myth: that they do stay. The truth is, women don't all stay. Up to 75 percent of those reporting abuse have left, permanently. But leaving has not exactly been the end of their problems: many have been followed, even stalked, harassed, and assaulted by former husbands or boyfriends. Many others have left only to return. The point, though, is that women don't just sit there and take it forever.

As for those women who don't pick up and leave, who stay or come back, the reasons have to do with the dynamics of domestic violence. "A woman living with a batterer," writes attorney Dawn Bradley Berry in her *Domestic Violence Sourcebook,* "is caught up in a very complex relationship that can trap her emotionally."

These involvements often start out as the "best relationship ever." The couple moves quickly into what seems like intimacy, and soon her life is all tangled up with his. They move in together, get married, and have babies, often so fast that everyone around them may wonder, "What's the rush?" He may be very jealous or just deeply interested in everything she does, but it seems he "really cares." The physical abuse may not start until she is pregnant, or after she has a child—and by then it's very difficult to get away. So it doesn't do any good for us to say, "Why don't the women just leave?" because the fact is they often can't—at least, not right away. What we need to ask is: "How can we help them to get free?"

The chief reason women don't "just leave" is fear. That fear is realistic: statistics show that a battered woman is more likely to be killed when she tries to leave than at any other time. (That is why it is important for her to carefully plan her escape; though this may sound reasonable to you, the reader, we may be asking that careful planning of a woman who's barely able to function by the time she decides she must leave.)

Another reason women stay is the kind of social conditioning specifically targeted at women. Many or most women get the message from childhood on that while they may have other interests, they will never be fulfilled unless they are married and have children. However, insisting that "that's all she's good for" is social conditioning of the worst kind. Women are held responsible for keeping the family together. The husband is to be the breadwinner, and the wife is to keep house and raise the kids. When a woman believes and accepts this conditioning, leaving an abusive husband means failing—not only as a mother or a wife, but as a woman, and as a human being. This is a disastrous premise that keeps women in violent homes.

Furthermore, women are told that "love conquers all." Many women hope that if they stick it out, the batterer will change. They remember how sweet he was when they were first introduced, and they're hoping that he will be that way again. Unfortunately, the charmer is not the real person, but just a side of his battering nature. (And the abuser fools not only the victim but many of the people around them. His co-workers, family, and friends may think she's nuts and he's just a sweetheart.)

Another point, made by Del Martin in her book *Battered Wives,* is that while society has long offered some solutions for battered women, upon closer examination we discover that these so-called solutions "actually exert pressure on her to endure her lot in the name of 'reconciliation.' " Martin argues that the criminal justice system, from your average cop to Supreme Court judges, needs to develop a new attitude toward domestic violence. Cops and judges tend to believe that it is better for a woman to "work it out" than to "give up." They don't see that this is not the issue. The issue is that the woman is with a monster. Social services must be tailored to fit what we know about family violence. Del Martin comments that the first thing these agencies need to do as a matter of policy is "formally acknowledge the existence of wife-beating as a social problem."

A woman may also endure abuse because, "for the sake of the children," she doesn't want to end her relationship with their father. This involves the deep sense of self-sacrifice which is taught in many religions, especially Christianity.

The fact is the batterer can use the children to keep control over his wife, as he sees that because of them she will not leave him. He may commit adultery repeatedly for years. That is psychological as well as sexual abuse, since his infidelity may expose her to sexually transmitted disease. But she will suffer the betrayal and degradation, as long as she can raise the children. She may not see or understand the level of damage done to her until after the children have grown up and left home, and the marriage has ended in divorce. (An abusive marriage with children will become a nightmarish divorce, though this is not a reason to stay. Rather, it's a reason to get out quickly so that both partners can recover and the children do not have to witness violence between parents.)

Another reason women stay is that it takes money to be able to leave. There are many more organizations nowadays ready to help with temporary shelter and counseling, but money is still a major issue. Women will endure physical abuse because they don't have enough money to leave, especially if they have children.

Why do these women stay? What is the deeper side of this trap? To answer these questions takes us into the psychological domain of domestic abuse. In 1979, psychologist Lenore Walker published *The Battered Woman,* which is now considered the classic initial research on this subject. (In other words, while the battering of women has gone on since the beginning of time, our current experts agree that the first serious work only came on the scene in 1979. This fact alone is evidence that inattention to the problem has allowed it to sink deep into our culture.) On the basis of interviews with 120 abused women, Walker developed her theory of what is now known as the battered woman syndrome.

It is here, entering into the psychological explanation of what batterers do, that we take a look at this sophisticated trap that captures or takes hostage so many women in their own homes. We discover what batterers do and how they do it. This is what is so important for everyone in our society to truly become familiar with. It is this above everything else that must become common knowledge in our culture if we are to stem and turn back the tide of domestic violence. Once this process is out in the open and more and more people are familiar with the way it works, the more difficult it will become for this to continue to go on. Right now, domestic violence persists, in part, because so many people still don't understand how it works and what happens. This is the section of the book you want to discuss with friends who want to understand the heart of domestic violence.

Jan Berliner Statman has written an excellent book entitled *The Battered Woman's Survival Guide,* which explains in a simple and lucid style what happens and how it happens. She observes:

A batterer can be hard to detect at the onset of a relationship, but . . . domestic violence builds in a clear, characteristic pattern. It is as if all batterers read the same imaginary handbook of techniques to help them promote violence. The woman is effectively brainwashed through a series of steps.

In *The Batterer,* Donald Dutton writes:

I have always been fascinated by these similarities among cyclical abusers' behavior patterns—even down to the words they use to humiliate women. It's as though they all attended a regimented school and studied the same curriculum. . . .

It is often asked why women stay in such damaging relationships. . . . These women unconsciously collude with their abusers in denial. Others become so beaten down that they seem to lose all will to care for themselves. . . . This strange loyalty [between a woman and her batterer] has been likened to the paradoxical bonds that form between hostages and victims in what is sometimes referred to as the Stockholm Syndrome. . . . We call this traumatic bonding.

Dr. Susan Forward, in her book *Men Who Hate Women and the Women Who Love Them*, remarks:

Ascribing good motives to people who are harming you is not limited to those in [battering] relationships. Sociologists first described this behavior and named it the Stockholm Syndrome after analyzing events that took place during a bank robbery in Sweden. Instead of hating the holdup men who had taken them hostage, the captives began to defend them. They projected positive motives onto their captors in an attempt to find safety in a hostile, life-threatening situation. Several of the people who had been held hostage by the robbers began to ex-

*hibit a combination of love and pity for them. . . . I am con-
vinced that for many women in [battering] relationships the
Stockholm Syndrome is in operation.*

The experts just quoted make two points that are very important
to understand and keep in mind. First, *batterers are following a program* (like a virus in a computer) that's in their head, complete with
a method of operation, a language, attitudes, actions and reactions,
and so on, that are distinct and identifiable. Second, *this program
acts as a classic form of brainwashing.* The victims are not only controlled in terms of what they can do or where they can go, but are
invaded to the very core of their being: the batterer wants their soul.

How did this program develop in the abuser's head? Dr. Susan
Forward explains that "once we begin to examine the forces that
drive the [batterer], we find that much of the abusive behavior is
a cover-up for his tremendous anxiety about women. . . . His normal needs to be close to a woman are mixed with fears that she
can annihilate him emotionally. He harbors a hidden belief that if
he loves a woman, she will then have the power to hurt him, to de-
prive him, to engulf him, and to abandon him."

It's this fundamental hidden belief that starts the program in the
life of a batterer and sets up the trap into which these men will
take women hostages. Many abusive men are very presentable, very
together on the outside, yet their inner life is governed by fear of
abandonment and rejection.

Abusive men also fear that they are "no good," "stupid," and
"bad"; such beliefs have been programmed into them through
heavy doses of shame. Where did this shame come from? Dr. Donald Dutton writes:

*In my research, evidence of shaming came out loud and clear:
Wife assaulters had experienced childhoods characterized by*

global attacks on their selfhood, humiliation, embarrassment, and shame. Their parents would often publicly humiliate them or punish them at random. Often such parents would say, "You're no good. You'll never amount to anything." The integrity of the child's self came under attack. . . . Indeed, I found that shaming experiences, primarily by the father, were strongly related to adult rage. . . . The results were so significant that, if I had to pick a single parental action that generated abusiveness in men, I would say it is being shamed by their fathers.

So the entrapment that so damages women begins in the childhood of a batterer, and *the single most catastrophic contribution is shaming by the father.* Dr. Dutton concludes, "Of course, fathers who shame their sons also tend to be physically abusive, so the boy not only sustains an attack on the self but also experiences abuse-modeling."

How do these men get from shamed young boys to adult men who batter women? Dr. Susan Forward writes that the batterer tries to reduce his sense of shame by belittling the woman he is with. She explains that the batterer "sets out, usually unconsciously, to make the woman in his life less powerful. He operates from the secret belief that if he can strip her of her self-confidence, she will be as dependent on him as he is on her." A batterer often operates unconsciously. He doesn't have direct control over what he is doing. Things that happened to him in his early years deeply influence his adult behavior. The good news is that we understand the process, pretty much. The bad news is that it isn't easy to heal these emotional wounds and they don't heal quickly.

What role does the batterer's mother play? Dr. Dutton writes: "A man's early relationship with his mother is the second key element in the evolution of the abusive personality."

When the mother is victimized at home, the child is traumatized for the rest of his life. A mother beaten down by a battering father becomes helpless; she loses her identity as an adult. This deprives the child of the needed maternal figure, starves him emotionally, and betrays him by leaving him vulnerable to abuse by the father. If this was not your experience, can you try to imagine being a little child and being forced to live this way year after year from the time you were born? It's hard to imagine, as if you'd been given a box of history books and asked to imagine what it was like to live in the twelfth century.

How does this experience affect a boy into his manhood? Generally speaking, the young boy begins to want to rescue his mother, but he faces impossible odds. She also fails to protect him from the physical and verbal abuses of the father. He feels betrayed by her because he is struggling to do things he can't, and because she doesn't protect him. This generates all kinds of fears and stresses that lead the boy to develop deep resentments at a very early age, resentments against pretty much everything and everyone—including, of course, himself. The boy is angry, humiliated, and enraged. Most of his needs as a child are ignored and repressed. He grows up emotionally malnourished, and consequently emotionally handicapped. He doesn't fully grow up emotionally. The result is that while in terms of years he is an adult, emotionally he remains a child.

He bears a deep rage and resentment toward his mother; these feelings are coupled with neediness, and he transfers them onto the women that he meets. *Paradoxically, he is both starving for affection and terrified of receiving it.* The more a woman tries to love him, the more he needs to run away. This undermines any possibility of a real loving relationship and often sets the stage for domestic violence.

At the start of this chapter, we asked why women stay in these relationships. We cleared up some myths and gave a more accurate reason: the women are trapped by a form of brainwashing. How does a batterer learn to brainwash his victim? The answer is to be found in the batterer's childhood. Batterers are survivors of horrible conditions that leave them prone to violence.

So what sets this trap in motion? First, these men are victimized as children. (This doesn't excuse their behavior, it simply explains it.) Second, often the whole process of trapping the woman is based on unconscious influences. The batterer has neither direct control over the trapping nor even a clear awareness that he is doing it.

What's the batterer's "M.O.," or modus operandi? In *The Battered Woman's Survival Guide*, Jan Statman explains the process clearly:

> *The batterer degrades her into believing that she is incompetent and incapable of managing the simplest task of daily life and interaction. When she expresses dissatisfaction or unhappiness, he convinces her she is to blame. He makes her believe that if she would only change, if she would only do as he says, their life together would be as perfect and as happy as they know it can be. He will create most, if not all, of the following circumstances:*

1. *Separation*

2. *Surveillance*

3. *Exhaustion and Hunger*

4. *Hostility and Paranoia*

5. *Chemical Dependence*

6. *Financial Dependence*

7. *Financial Deprivation*

8. *Discredit*

9. *Insecurity*

10. *Battering*

11. *A Cycle of Violence*

12. *Sexual Abuse*

13. *Guilt and Denial*

While the man may be the victim of childhood abuse and neglect, do not make the mistake of pitying him, for he is also a terrorist, without real emotions—often without a conscience—and he is a threat to his partner's life and that of their children. What's important is to get better acquainted with each of these tactics in the entrapment process of domestic violence. They are listed here in their order of highest probability.

• **SEPARATION:** Once he has her, his first objective, consciously or unconsciously, is to separate her from relatives and friends. Isolation has always been the first step in the brainwashing process. The abuser will isolate a woman in many ways, and it will not happen overnight. But notice that she has suddenly been separated from family and friends. He is likely to move her to another city; jobs are usually the best-sounding excuse. That's **step 1.**

• **SURVEILLANCE:** Control is the big issue here. The abuser wants to know everything about the woman. When they were dating, she probably found that charming, but the ugly truth is revealed. He moves into establishing control through demands to hear about every moment of her day. Charming concern turns into ugly interrogation and the frightening realization that something is wrong with this man. The woman must account to him for every phone call, every person she talked to that day, and so on. He may show up at her job without warning. This is surveillance, not romantic pursuit. That's **step 2.**

- **EXHAUSTION AND HUNGER:** In behavior control or brainwashing during times of war, the next step a captor takes to gain maximum control over his prisoner is sensory disorientation, followed by sensory deprivation. The abuser will work on her to disorient her and to weaken her physically. The tool that most effectively accomplishes this is sleep disruption and deprivation. If you are a prisoner of war and your captor wants to brainwash you, he knows that keeping you from sleeping is the single best way to undermine your mind, your personality, and your capacity to escape. That will wipe you out with startling efficacy. No sleep (or constantly disrupted sleep) in combination with no food can weaken you quickly to the point that you experience a personality meltdown. Sleep deprivation is **step 3.**

- **HOSTILITY AND PARANOIA:** He starts to turn violent toward the woman. First he uses verbally abusive language, then escalates to throwing food, smashing small objects, grabbing her, ripping her clothes, and threatening her and her children. By these actions he proves that he is, and will continue to be, a batterer. The victim will remember how charming he is in public but will be seeing this entirely other person in private. The charming person is just a decoy. The real person is acting out his nature in violence. This is a batterer. Men like this sometimes kill women. **Step 4.**

- **CHEMICAL DEPENDENCE:** The abuser may try to get his victim hooked on something. If he can get her to use alcohol or drugs to drown out what he is doing to her, this will serve his overall plan. The victim may be able to forget her problems while under the influence, but unfortunately, she's also digging herself deeper in the hole. If she can, she should get herself to a Twelve Step meeting right away. **Step 5.**

- **FINANCIAL DEPENDENCE:** Remember, the batterer is after complete control. He wants his victim's body, mind, and spirit. One major means of control is money. Money is power. The abuser will come up with all kinds of reasons why his partner should leave her job and stay home. It doesn't matter what ploy he uses; his objective is always the same. She is now completely dependent on him for money. **Step 6.**

- **FINANCIAL DEPRIVATION:** A woman can be with a rich man or a poor man; if he is a batterer, it makes no difference. A woman may be penniless while living with a wealthy man. He will withhold money from her and demand a detailed accounting of where every penny has been spent. She will always have problems paying household bills. Another area of control is transportation. He may arrange things so that they only have one car, which he pays for and he has to drive to work. **Step 7.**

- **DISCREDIT:** When she quits her job, he will find a way to make sure she doesn't or can't go back. He will either disgrace her in front of her former employer or work directly on her, accusing her of having affairs with her boss or co-workers. If she has money before they meet, he will inveigle her into a business deal to drain her financially. He will steal her credit cards, purchase things in her name, and then steal the mail to keep the purchases secret. He will sabotage her tax returns if he can. He will infiltrate and manipulate every aspect of her finances. **Step 8.**

• **INSECURITY:** As all these tactics work to take hold of the woman from many angles, she starts to lose all sense that she is in control of her life. Now a deep sense of insecurity appears in every aspect of her life. **Step 9.**

• **BATTERING:** Once all these tactics are completely in place, the woman is completely at the mercy of the batterer, and her life now belongs to him.

Episodes of battering can start with arguments, which may or may not make sense, but batterers need no excuse. They may wake up the wife or girlfriend and beat her senseless when all she was doing was sleeping. Reasoning with this man is over; he has established the perfect environment, in which his deepest, darkest, most crazed ambitions, fears, and rages can be let loose. The woman is now a lightning rod for all his repressed humiliation and rage. **Step 10.**

• **A CYCLE OF VIOLENCE:** Experts agree that a battered woman lives in a three-phase cycle. She soon learns to identify the signs of imminent battering—to recognize the signs of the coming storm. In the first phase, she can feel the tension building. Most battered women describe this phase of life with the batterer as "walking on eggshells." In the second phase, the violence begins and explodes, until he gets it out of his system. The violence may last an hour, several hours, or several days. He can become so completely possessed with it that he dissociates, and afterward literally doesn't remember what he did to her. Finally, in the third phase, the "honeymoon" phase, the batterer reverts to his charming self. He promises to change and he gives the victim gifts. He is not doing this for her, but for himself, setting up the groundwork for phase one to start again a little later. And so on, and so on. (The next chapter deals with this three-phase cycle to give you a perspective from inside the storm.) **Step 11.**

• **SEXUAL DEMANDS, SEXUAL VIOLENCE, AND SEXUAL PECULIARITIES:** What the abuser wants sexually has little to do with what the woman needs. Such a man does not know how to show true affection or love. Sex on demand; rape; brutal, violent, and degrading acts may be what he demands instead. He can be gentle, exciting, and delightful in bed on one occasion and a vicious, raging brute the next. He may like to mutilate her. He may force her to have sex with other men. Some abusive men turn their wives or girlfriends into prostitutes, then take the money they earn. A batterer may force his wife or girlfriend to pose for nude photographs, which he will use later for blackmail or actually send to relatives and friends. He may accuse her of being a bisexual, a lesbian, or a crazed nymphomaniac. **Step 12.**

• **GUILT AND DENIAL:** It doesn't seem that someone could learn to become completely helpless, but this is what domestic violence does to a woman. It brainwashes her into accepting herself as a victim. The process goes right to the core of the personality and changes the self-image of the woman. She comes to believe that her life is over, and that this is her lot in life. This means that her will to change, or hope, is gone. The guilt and denial work together to make her more isolated. If confronted by a friend or relative, she will deny that there is anything wrong. She will lie to everyone about her injuries—even to doctors who recognize their nature. **Step 13.**

• **LEARNED HELPLESSNESS:** "In insidious ways," writes Jan Statman, "the woman is thus 'brainwashed.' Her independence is eroded. Her perception of reality is distorted. Her self-confidence is undermined. She learns how to be helpless. She learns to be a victim." **Step 14.**

A battered woman's friends and family may not understand why she will not leave. They won't be able to figure out why she will not ask for help. They haven't understood the steps just explained. Essentially, the victim is not at all the person they have always known. *All that's left is the exterior.* Her personality and her mind have been assaulted so deeply that she has been co-opted and is no longer in control of her decision-making faculties. She has been brainwashed into thinking that she is repulsive, useless, brainless, and a waste of space. Though physically she may be with her family and friends, she is living in a completely different reality.

What's the answer? The victim must be encouraged to seek help; if she refuses, the children, at least, must be protected, because the abuser may kidnap or kill them. Abuse happens every day in America, twenty-four hours a day. It happens to nice women like your friend or your daughter. Her family or friends must first realize that they are in the presence of a battered woman. They must do whatever they can to teach her there is a way out. The second section of this book will help the victim find her own way out of the abusive relationship. Encourage her without forcing your solutions on her.

In the next chapter, we will look at life inside the cycle of domestic violence.

Chapter 4

What Happens in the Violent Relationship?

The violence that battered women live with is beginning to be understood by experts who work with victims and batterers. How important is it for us to learn about this violence? There are approximately 4 million reported cases a year, and perhaps nine or ten times as many unreported cases. As one activist says, every battered woman stands alone, isolated, and without a support system in place; we must become a nation of people who understand this kind of violence. Lou Brown told us once that though more women were turning to shelters and leaving abusive relationships than ever before, he felt he had failed. Why? Because there were long waiting lists for shelters; because courts don't give women the protection they need; and because battered women have long-term needs that are not met by shelters. This book will do more than teach you about domestic violence. It will allow you to help victims directly and indirectly, which is the single most important "cure" for domestic violence. If you understand the causes of violence, you will be participating in what experts agree is the single most important part of the cure: education.

In her book *Terrifying Love: Why Battered Women Kill and How Society Responds,* Lenore Walker writes that the "cycle of violence must be understood if we are to develop a genuine understanding of the dynamics of domestic violence in our society and of the psychology of battered women."

In the last chapter, we answered the question why women stay in these horrible relationships: they are trapped by a complex form of brainwashing, and they need help in getting out. We looked at the process that traps their souls. We identified some of the tactics used by batterers. We studied how they learned to do this to women.

In this chapter, we will step into the eye of the storm. We will describe what the woman sees and feels as the abuser's rage builds, explodes, and then subsides—only to start all over again. Two concepts in this chapter must be discussed by people everywhere. These two concepts are the key to understanding domestic violence. The first is Lenore Walker's "cycle of violence," and the second is psychologist Martin Seligman's "learned helplessness."

By explaining domestic violence we want to demythologize it. When we don't understand something, we build up all kinds of fantastic scenarios; this does not help us get to the truth. As we seek out understanding, it becomes clear what we can do to help. This is why we want to get to the truth of a problem: so that we can find the right answers.

We hope it's clear to you after reading the last chapter that women do not stay in these relationships because they are weak or because they enjoy the violence. It should also be clearer to you why women will not seek help when they need it, even when their lives are in clear danger. All around us are people trapped in these relationships. With an understanding of how violence operates on the battered woman, we can make some intelligent choices regarding this often life-and-death issue. Even more important, we can keep ourselves from misunderstanding the situation and making the wrong choices, choices that will contribute to the woman's further abuse. Together, we can change things.

Lenore Walker is considered by many experts to be the leading authority in this new field. In *Terrifying Love* she says: "Even though it [the cycle of violence] does not occur in all battering relationships, it was reported to occur in two-thirds of the sixteen hundred incidents in our studies on battered women."

Although our common sense may suggest that battered women live with random violence, and that the batterer just explodes from time to time, or on the other hand that battered women are constantly being abused and that the violence is nonstop, *our common sense is plain wrong.* The violence is neither random nor constant. It's *predictable.* This understanding means that we can help the women. It also means that we can help batterers, in some instances.

What kind of pattern can be seen in this violence? The pattern most identified by experts was initially identified by Walker in her 1979 book, *The Battered Woman,* for which she interviewed 120 women. What she said then has proven to be true over and over again:

> *One of the most striking discoveries in the interviews was of a definite battering cycle these women experience. Understanding this cycle is very important if we are to learn how to stop or prevent battering incidents. This cycle also helps explain how battered women become victimized, how they fall into learned helplessness behavior, and why they do not attempt escape.*
>
> *The battering cycle appears to have three distinct phases, which vary in both time and intensity for the same couple and between different couples. These are: (1) the tension-building phase; (2) the explosion or acute battering incident; and (3) the calm, loving respite. So far, I have been unable to estimate how long a couple will remain in any one phase, nor can I predict how long a couple will take to complete a cycle.*

The first thing to understand about what domestic violence is like for the woman being battered is that, as Lenore Walker has said, it is "a cycle of violence," with a pattern of three phases. Battered women are often—not always—able to judge where they are in the cycle and when an abuser is likely to explode. About two-thirds of violent couples follow this pattern.

Phase One

This is the tension-building phase. The man becomes edgy, critical, and just plain irritable. He doesn't need a reason to feel this way. She knows what's coming, and she may try to pacify him. That's a waste of time. (In some instances it actually triggers the second phase.) Being around the abuser during this phase is like walking on eggshells. Basically, the woman is damned if she says something, because he may take it as a challenge, which will set him off; and she's damned if she says nothing, because he feels that she is withdrawing and not giving him the attention he wants. (Bottom line: he wants to control her.)

As he gets more and more tense, there is the inevitable escalation, starting with small incidents involving yelling, slapping, and calling her names—"whore" or "slut." She may try to pacify him, but he's on to her quickly, escalating with his own techniques for rendering her helpless and releasing his rage. If she acts nice and sweet, he feels she's giving him license to let her have it. If she challenges him, she's gone. This can go on for days; it can even go on for years.

Some women actually get so edgy that they finally do or say just the thing that will "make him lose it." This is not to say that the woman's in control, but only that many victims feel that if they get that part over, go through the violence, they'll be back to "normal." In Part Two, written for the victim, we will show how she can use phase one to plan her escape and lower the level of violence. This period is when she can leave; it's usually impossible to go during the explosion phase. But her fear will keep her in until she is strong enough to leave and has a way out.

Phase Two

He "loses it" and gets violent. Some women experience emotional brutality, but usually the violence is physical; it can lead to her death. The rage is blind and senseless. The man is transformed into a madman. A woman will describe her husband as physically transformed: his eyes bulge; the pupils are dilated; he is seething with rage. Some men rage until they nearly pass out, while others become calmer and calmer as they pulverize everything and everyone in sight. These are some of our solid and upright citizens— civic leaders and professionals who seem to be examples of success when they're out in society, and "regular guys" who seem to be very gentle and kind.

It's important to realize that most women who kill their batterers do so before he gets to this stage. They know what is coming, and they kill him because they believe he will kill them. But most battered women don't kill their husbands, and most batterers do not kill their victims.

Phase Three

After the brutality, Mr. Hyde reverts to the smart and charming Dr. Jekyll: the psychopath disappears and is replaced by an often sweet, loving, and very contrite man. Unless you see this transformation, it is hard to believe that the two can be the same man. By this time the battered woman is in such a physical and mental state that she is putty in his hands. While he acts sweet, psychologists believe he is actually working his psychological tactics, digging the claws of control more deeply into her soul. He cons her into thinking that only a loving woman could put up with this level of abuse, that she's the key to his emotional well-being. He wants her to feel that he depends on her for forgiveness; at the same time, she thinks that this is how she'll get back the "real" man. She believes that his violent side is not the real person; rather, the "sweet" side is. She doesn't understand that the reverse is true: the sweet side is a con, a lie, a more sophisticated tactic to get deeper into her and suck the life out of her. This is precisely what these sick men live for. It is important that batterers be seen for what they are. These men kill helpless women by the thousands. They brutalize pregnant women and often cause miscarriages or even kill the mother. They lead some women to suicide or murder.

But this is the best time for her to leave him. The magic window of opportunity is during phase one or between phases two and three. Before he gets her back into bed, she must leave. The part between the "honeymoon," phase three, and the tension-building stage, phase one, is often the only time in their lives they are happy together. The kids are happy, the world seems perfect. It is really hard for her to leave in that period.

When the explosion comes, she may call 911, but often by the time the police arrive, the man is calm and back in control. Maybe the house is a mess; the woman is probably hysterical. Whom are the police, if they're uninformed about domestic abuse, going to believe? They will see a sobbing woman, a calm man, and a messy house. If there are children, they may be crying. This is where education is so important. Rather than arresting the husband or boyfriend, the police may arrest *her* if the husband insists that she was the violent person. They may tell her that if she insists on his arrest, she will have to go to the police station, while the kids will be put into foster care. Such episodes actually happen, though education is changing that.

One thing you can do right now is find out what arrest policy and training program your police department has. If it does not have a domestic violence program, insist that one be started. Write letters to the editor of your local paper and speak with others about the matter. Police are among the most important people in the battle against violence. They must learn about it, and the law must provide for the arrest of a batterer when the woman reaches out for help.

As this cycle repeats itself, self-deception, "denial," takes hold of the woman. She will tell herself that this beating will be the last—that now, finally, he's serious and will change. But unless something else changes—unless, for instance, there's intervention by a group of friends or by family members from outside the home—the cycle will start again, and the abuse will simply escalate.

What makes the victim unable to seek help on her own? The answer lies in a phenomenon called learned helplessness. When you understand it, you will not let yourself give up easily when the battered woman doesn't respond as common sense tells you she should. In other words, if you offer to help her but she flatly turns you down even though her life is clearly in great danger, that shouldn't surprise you—once you understand what learned helplessness is. In his book *The Batterer,* Dr. Donald Dutton explains that the victim of domestic violence has no place to run and no place to hide. The victim becomes convinced of this—and when she is, all she can do is just emotionally lie down and play dead. She has lost hope and the will to run. Dutton describes the kind of experiment that psychologist Martin Seligman did to study this phenomenon:

> [He] experimented with dogs that he placed in a similar neg-
> ative situation. He put them in harnesses so they could not es-
> cape electric shock to their paws. When Seligman removed the
> harnesses and reapplied the shocks, the dogs just lay down and
> took them. They didn't try to escape, even when it was possi-
> ble. This behavioral unresponsiveness is called learned help-
> lessness.

Women trapped in domestic violence often behave similarly. They
have an emotional response as well. Unfortunately, an abused
woman knows that if she says anything she will be severely punished. What are her options? She must swallow her feelings.

Dr. Mary Susan Miller in her book *No Visible Wounds*, writes
that "Even those professionals who oppose the learned-
helplessness theory admit that a psychologically abused woman
often falls into a clinical depression that produces similar symp-
toms: loss of initiative, resignation, inability to handle even the sim-
plest daily chores."

What happens next? The abused woman believes that she is
held captive and there's no way out. She feels responsible for her
troubles. She can't believe her life has come to this, and she starts
to wonder if she did something to bring this on herself. She loses
all sense of control over the smallest things in her life—for example, whom she can talk to and when. Her sense of dignity is wiped
out by the psychological effects of the battering. She learns to dis-
sociate (seeing herself as if out of her body, looking down from
above upon herself and her abuser) from this horror as a means
of coping.

How far can this go? As the abuse goes on and intensifies, she
will become increasingly despondent, withdrawn, even suicidal.
Sometimes, in one last desperate act, a battered woman may kill
her abuser. But even if she kills him, at first she may not believe

that he is dead. She may run into another room and stay there for hours, thinking the batterer is playing dead, waiting for her to come back so he can jump up and beat her some more. Such a woman no longer believes that anything she does can harm the all-powerful and invincible batterer. She has learned this from years of being powerless.

Now you have read enough about domestic violence to equip yourself with some important tools. This chapter taught you two critical concepts, which you can discuss with other people: domestic violence involves (1) *a cycle of violence* that leads to (2) *learned helplessness.*

Share these ideas with friends. People must become aware of this information. Throughout this book, we mention the best literature currently available on this plague. Give those books, and this one, as gifts. Stimulate conversation. Every time you discuss domestic violence with other people, you are shining a little light on the ignorance that hides in the dark. We need to get this subject out in the open.

This book will also go beyond just talking about domestic violence. See the Epilogue to learn what you can do locally. The first step comes down to you and me: we must choose to do something. The choice to do nothing is exactly what makes the problem worse.

Chapter 5

What Can I Do to Help a Battered Woman?

You suspect that a woman friend is being abused. Or you know for sure she is being abused. Maybe a woman has told you she is being abused. Perhaps you hardly know her, yet she has come to you and revealed this terrible secret in her life. What are you going to do? What can you do to help her?

First, read through this entire book. Know what you're up against; otherwise, you're very likely to say or do the wrong thing (usually by trying to do too much). You can help save this woman's life without doing anything beyond what you do in your life now. In other words, you will not be required to don a red cape and fly through the air faster than a speeding bullet in order to whisk her away to safety. No one is going to ask you to walk on water or part the Red Sea. Sit yourself down quietly and read this book all the way through. Get past any commonsense but wrong ideas you have about domestic violence and act, not react, on the basis of the knowledge you get from this book. (If you've just picked up this book, turned to the table of contents, and then turned directly to this chapter, start from the beginning. You must read this whole book before you can help her. We wish we didn't have to tell you this, but it's the truth. If you don't know what this book says, we can almost guarantee that you will fail.)

If she is ready to leave, tell her you want to help her and *give her this phone number:* **1-800-799-SAFE**. This is the twenty-four-hour National Domestic Violence Hotline. Ask her if she wants to use your phone. Make sure she has a pen and paper, since she will get referrals to shelters and hotlines in your area. She must begin to plan. Have her read Part Two of this book, because it is for her.

If you're a man, and a woman has come to you for help, or you want to approach her because you think she needs help, be careful. The fact that you are a man and she is a woman can complicate matters. When you start listening to a woman who's going through so much suffering, she may consciously or unconsciously start to cling to you emotionally. She may even become very stuck on you. You don't need to discuss this with her the first meeting, but simply try to keep it in mind. You may want to ask her if she has a woman friend she is talking to also. If so, encourage her to share the deeper things with that friend. Do say that you'll be glad to help get her all the support information she needs by calling local shelters, the police, the sheriff, the church, the prosecutor's office, the public library, state and local domestic violence coalitions, and other general crisis or self-help lines. This is vital and necessary support. If she has no woman friend to talk to, don't back away; follow the procedure below and keep in mind what we have just said.

From this point on, as a friend to this victim of domestic violence, you must let staying in touch be up to her. Always let her suggest when she wants to meet next. Do ask her whether she'd like to meet (she may be too shy to ask), but don't impose a place or time. Be clear in your mind what you are willing to do to help and where you need to draw the line. Stay within these boundaries.

First Conversation

You are going to begin by doing the least in order to accomplish the most. This sounds like a trick saying. It's not. The least you can do is *listen* to her. That's also the *most important thing fo* initially and throughout her escape.

How do you deal with a woman who you suspect is k tered, but who has not brought up the subject? Perhaps you think she may be keeping it a secret from everyone. First, it is important to note that the majority of battered women today *are* keeping it a secret. Second, after having read the previous chapters you know that if she is a battered woman it doesn't matter what she looks like on the outside (i.e., a complete failure or a total success); battering affects women across all income levels. Third, you understand that if she is a battered woman the context of domestic violence in which she lives has brainwashed her: she may not even realize that she is a battered woman. If that sounds crazy to you, it is. But what it means is that she may not feel she wants or needs your help; she may flatly reject a direct offer of it. So just coming out and asking her is not a good idea.

How do you encourage a battered woman to open up and seek help if she doesn't already realize she needs it? You have in your hands this book. Start by just meeting with her (if that is possible) and discussing this book. Talk to her with the attitude that you're just now discovering this extraordinary phenomenon in American society. Express surprise at how widespread and secret this is. Read her some statistics from the first chapter. Talk to her about how people have all these misconceptions about what domestic violence is, about what batterers do and what they're supposed to look like. If possible, take the book and put it in her hands, and let her look at the list about what batterers do (page 36) and read it by herself.

Then all you can do is watch and let her respond. *Don't force the issue.* If she doesn't want to talk about it, do not bring it up until she does. This may take days. She may decide to talk about it, but not with you. But this conversation with you may have changed her mind about telling someone else. In other words, you may have planted a seed and someone else will get to water it.

If she begins to talk about her situation, this may be a life-changing breakthrough moment for her. Don't blow it. Just remain quiet and let her tell you about it, in her own way, at her own speed. The only thing you want to do is ask questions, if you have to, to help you understand what she is describing.

It is vital that you not say anything bad about the batterer. She will rush to his defense. Keep the focus on her and what she needs to do. You are not a professional. You can, however, lead her to people who are.

Whatever you do, do not say you'll have a talk with the batterer, or that you'll call the police. Be her friend, guide her to resources, encourage her to get strong inside of herself so *she* can change her life.

There are other things you don't want to do at this point.

First, *do not doubt her* for one moment. Believe that she is telling you the truth. Experts tell us that women very, very rarely make these stories up.

Second, do not be surprised if she is a little incoherent. Do not ask questions in an attempt to help her remember any sequence of events. Simply let her talk. Even if she is wrong about something that you remember differently, just let her talk. *Do not try to correct her.* In the future, there will be time to set history right. Remember that you are dealing with someone who may be deeply scarred by the horrors and countless torments she's been enduring. She may have been terrorized by physical beatings. She may be living in a constant climate of fear; her abuser may use elaborate mental tortures that leave no visible wounds. The latter can often be even worse than physical beatings. It takes expertise to deal with psychological scars.

Third, *remember the Jekyll-and-Hyde syndrome.* You shouldn't be surprised if the batterer always seems perfectly together and in public looks like a model citizen. This is usually the case. (Of course, the fact that a man is a model citizen doesn't mean that he is a batterer.) If what she is saying seems impossible, let your objections go; just let her describe her situation in detail. Simply accept and believe what she is saying. Do not raise the issue of whether or not you think he might be capable of this. Accept what she says about the man, no matter how bad it is. Let her get it all out in the open.

At the end of this initial conversation *tell her that you believe her.* Say to her: "I believe ALL you've told me. I believe you."

Also—and this is very important—she needs to hear from you repeatedly that you know that *battered women do not cause the battering.* Say it to her repeatedly, "You didn't cause this. He had this insanity inside him before you ever met him."

This is the truth, and she needs to hear it because the batterer has been working on her mind, hammering into her the idea that the battering is her fault. This is a core aspect of the insanity of this problem: he beats the life out of her and he keeps telling her that it's her fault.

When the conversation ends, ask her whether and when she would like to meet again to talk with you. You may want to tell her that you will help her in any way that she wants.

Afterward, consider what has happened and what you've done. This woman has been living a hellish existence. It took a lot of courage for her to talk to you. She has done you a great honor and offered you a great privilege by simply sharing her situation with you. She has trusted you. Trust is precious in this day and age; you can repay hers by remembering a key principle here: *confidentiality.* You must not repeat to another soul what was said between you. Make the commitment to go to the grave with this information. The only exception is if her children are being physically abused. Then you call child protective services or 1-800-4-A-CHILD to report the abuse. Failure to keep confidentiality will constitute further abuse of this poor woman who has trusted you. Do not tell anyone, no matter who it is, what she has shared with you. You can ask her permission to talk with someone, but never assume that you have it. This is absolutely vital for the battered woman's recovery.

What else has happened? The battered woman has taken her first step to freedom, and you have become her agent of freedom. Your primary role will be to listen, to help her by allowing her to speak with you. It may seem like a small thing, but it's far more significant than you may at first realize. You are giving her a ray of hope when she has known only the deepest darkness. Be a friend. Listen to her. Keep everything she says absolutely confidential. Unless you have her permission, never tell anyone anything she has said to you—not anyone, not even her relatives or other friends. Much damage is done when people betray confidentiality.

Does this mean that no one else is to know? The support of others will be necessary; others will eventually have to be told. The issue here is trust. Do not violate hers. She will tell you whom you can speak to, and when. Always reassure her that you will not discuss this with anyone else. Not your closest friend, not even your spouse.

What happens next? First, patience is essential. Do not be surprised if you have a few meetings with the woman and things get worse but she is not ready to leave the abuser. *Do not rush her to leave him.* It is critical for you to realize that leaving is dangerous: that is when women are likely to suffer the worst injuries and when they are most likely to be killed. It is natural for someone in your position (a caring friend) to want her to leave quickly; just hold on to that reaction. You want to act, not react. She needs a plan that will work. Once she leaves, she's not coming back. Once she leaves, a whole new set of challenges will come her way. These need to be thought through *before* she leaves.

Second Conversation

You should have done some of the legwork mentioned above—namely, you need to have called the following:

• National Domestic Violence Hotline (1-800-799-SAFE or, for the hearing impaired, 1-800-787-3224)

• local shelters

• the sheriff or police (or both)

• the prosecutor's office

• state and local domestic violence coalitions

• other general crisis or self-help lines

• the church, synagogue, or mosque

• the public library

Ask each one question: "In a case of domestic violence, what do you do?" Let them explain it to you. Make clear notes, including the name of the agency, its phone number, and the name of the person you spoke with. Your friend's life is chaotic enough, so give her the information in a clear, well-organized, and if possible, typed format. Whenever possible, go to the agencies and meet the people who deal with domestic violence. Face-to-face meetings are important for something like this. We also recommend that you read the books we mention.

It is important not to do too much. A battered woman has been put down so much she may feel she can't do anything herself. If you try to fix her life, she will not be able to develop confidence that she herself is in control of her life. Generally, do encourage her to get into a support group, to read books about the problem, and to read Part Two of this book. Tell her you'll be there for her, but remember: *she* must be the one who decides when she leaves. You can answer her questions by saying, "I'll find out—or better yet, why don't you call a shelter and ask?" *Don't be a crutch for her.* Be a person who loves her, who knows about the problems she faces, and who encourages her to find her inner power again. Many people who work with abuse victims talk about "taking back your power." It's an important idea, because we all have some inner part of ourselves that can think, choose, have attitudes and beliefs. That place is where our engine is, and she must take possession of it again. Only she can do that.

You should know that women who've discussed their ordeals have all expressed the deepest thanks to the people who helped them in their escape. She may or may not be able to express those thanks directly, but she will never forget all you did for her. She will remember it the rest of her life.

Chapter 6

What Is Nonphysical Abuse?

Millions of women in America are beaten with blows that leave no wounds. This abuse is an aspect of the kind that leaves women with bruises, black eyes, and broken bones, and sends them to our emergency rooms and mortuaries. Nonphysical abuse is the most hidden kind of domestic violence and is the kind that most thoroughly paralyzes its victims—so thoroughly that a woman may take years to realize what's been happening to her. On page 63 we give you a list of questions from the Battered Women's Task Force of the New York State Coalition Against Domestic Violence so that you can quickly assess whether or not you are a victim of this type of domestic violence.

The most important book to date on this subject is Dr. Mary Susan Miller's *No Visible Wounds: Identifying Nonphysical Abuse of Women by Their Men.* The millions of women in America who suffer nonphysical abuse are controlled by deliberate intimidation, emotional and sexual manipulation or withdrawal, humiliation, restriction of money, and isolation. While they cannot deny their deep anguish, fear, guilt, and confusion, because this cruelty inflicts no visible wounds, these women often do not make the connection with the word *abuse.*

A woman may stay for years with a man who practices psychological abuse. He doesn't have to lay a hand on her to be actively practicing abuse: all he has to do is twist her mind so that she submits to his will without a fight. She will feel that she's losing her mind but will not be able to define how. She will even think that if she confides in family or friends, they'll tell her that she's wrong: her husband's not doing this, she's going crazy all on her own.

Dr. Mary Susan Miller writes:

> *It is difficult for a man who punches a woman or throws her into a wall to not know that he is an abuser. It is equally difficult for a woman who sustains a black eye and body bruises not to know she has been abused, although both of them find rationales to avoid reality. However, the subtle manifestations of nonphysical abuse usually escape acknowledgment—at least for a long period of time. Although a man can't help being consciously aware of depriving a woman of money or social contacts or of drumming into her that she is stupid and crazy, he can be consciously unaware that what he is doing is legally abusive. Similarly, a woman, cognizant that she is systematically being made miserable, may not recognize what is happening as abuse. The netherworld environment in which they both live, therefore, keeps abuse alive and thriving until—and if—the woman steps into the reality of the real world by demanding a halt.*

Remember that until twenty-five years ago, the term "battered woman" didn't even exist. As for psychological abuse, society too often accepts it as part of the normal problems in a marriage. Society even encourages some abusive attitudes, since women are often taught to submit. This is why it is so difficult for emotionally abused women to understand and realize their abuse. Until now.

A man can abuse a woman nonphysically without hating her. We assume that a man abusing a woman is going to be in rage, foaming at the mouth like a rabid dog, ready to pulverize her. Reality is different from this comic-book image. A man can abuse a woman while loving her—but the love is sick. In other words, he thinks it's love; she thinks it's the only love he's capable of giving her; and really it's not love at all. While the relationship will not be physically violent, it will reduce the woman to an emotional cripple, starved for affection and convinced that she's lucky to have this man. That's the insanity of the situation: *he takes everything from her, and she thinks she's lucky to have him.*

How can you know if you are a victim of nonphysical abuse? Read the following nineteen questions and answer them truthfully. Regardless of how you might answer them in front of anyone else, we encourage you to answer them truthfully to yourself. As explained above, these questions were put together by the Battered Women's Task Force of the New York State Coalition Against Domestic Violence (they also appear in Dr. Miller's book); notice that only numbers 1, 13, and 14 relate to *physical* violence against women.

Does your partner:

1. *hit, punch, slap, shove, or bite you?*

2. *threaten to hurt you or your children?*

3. *threaten to hurt friends or family members?*

4. *have sudden outbursts of anger or rage?*

5. *behave in an overprotective manner?*

6. *become jealous without reason?*

7. *prevent you from seeing family or friends?*

8. *prevent you from going where you want, when you want?*

9. *prevent you from working or attending school?*

10. *destroy personal property or sentimental items?*

11. *deny you access to family assets such as bank accounts, credit cards, or the car?*

12. *control all finances and force you to account for what you spend?*

13. *force you to have sex against your will?*

14. *force you to engage in sexual acts you do not enjoy?*

15. *insult you or call you derogatory names?*

16. *use intimidation or manipulation to control you or your children?*

17. *humiliate you in front of your children?*

18. *turn minor incidents into major arguments?*

19. *abuse or threaten to abuse pets?*

The Battered Women's Task Force says: "If you answered yes to one or more of the above . . . you might be abused." How many times did you find yourself answering yes?

In a recent conversation, a woman one of us has known for three years explained that in her twenty-five-year marriage she never saw what her husband did as abuse. Divorced three years ago, she recently read some of the books we mention, and she started to recognize, for the first time, that she was abused by her former husband. That is, she now sees, for the first time, that she was abused for a quarter of a century. This is the nature of this highly deceptive form of domestic violence: *women can be trapped in it for years without coming to their senses, without realizing that they are being victimized.* Don't be surprised if after you read the nineteen questions above, your reaction was: "What? He's been doing these things to me for years. You mean to tell me that this is really considered abuse? I thought abuse was when he hit you." Abuse can be physical, but almost always it begins with nonphysical abuse.

Nonphysical abuse is horrible because it erases the victim's feelings and makes her feel like a dumb, numb nonperson. A man can beat the daylights out of a woman, leaving her with broken bones, bruises all over her body, and blood soaking her clothes—and with a feeling of emptiness and worthlessness that goes even deeper than physical pain. The woman feels like trash. That does something to her very soul, and it's not going to heal as fast as the broken bones, the bruises, and the cuts. The body heals much more quickly than the soul.

Why do these men do it? It's very important to understand that the reason isn't that they enjoy inflicting pain. This isn't sadism. *Their motive is control.* This sick need underlies everything they do in the relationship, and it will make them do bizarre things. One man, whose ex-wife was coming to pick up a car that the divorce had granted her, took the car to a body shop and had all the glass and the upholstery removed. He told his ex-wife that vandals had stripped the car. What gave him away was that the glass and the upholstery had been perfectly and neatly removed. What kind of vandal is neat? This was the ex-husband's attempt to convince himself that he still had some measure of control over at least one aspect of her life. Typically, abusive men cannot control their unconscious need to control the women in their lives.

A woman who suffers nonphysical abuse comes to believe that no matter how hard she tries to please her man, she'll fail—not because he's asking something unreasonable but because she can't do anything right: she's not smart enough, and the relationship is bad because of her and her stupidity. Emotionally abusive men wear women down with this approach. Whenever she does something, or fails to do something else, he will always find something wrong with it. He doesn't have to find something seriously wrong with it, just something wrong. He'll never find anything right, just dig into her at every opportunity. Every fault, every mistake he can name just keeps building up the pile, the ever-growing mountain of mistakes that he's found in everything she does. This buries her, and lifts him up to the sense of complete control that is all he wants. He lives to put her down. That's his mission in life.

Having started by putting her down at home, he will go on to do it in public. As Dr. Mary Miller writes, "Abuse never—and I use the word *never* fully aware of its pitfalls—goes away [by itself] . . . Name-calling grows into public humiliation, isolation, and eventually threats, at which level a union may continue until death do them part; on the other hand, threats may become the reality of beatings and murder."

The emotionally abusive man may go from embarrassing his victim in front of her friends by criticizing what she wears, how she talks, even how she eats, to accusing her of having lovers. He may graduate to stalking her, even following her when she is just meeting a female friend. Dr. Miller tells of a man who was stalking his wife and saw her walk up to a man and speak with him. The husband came up from behind them and was ready to just lay into her when the man turned around to face him. It was her father.

Another type of abuse these men practice is the silent treatment. When the woman responds to one of his accusations or fabrications and the circumstances are clearly on her side, one way for an emotionally abusive man to take control is to walk away or pout and not speak to her for days at a time. This tactic—which is especially ugly because it's an invisible assault directed at the soul of the woman—makes her feel undesirable and unneeded. And without any communication she can't gauge where he's at and what he is thinking. What will he do next? This instills tension and fear inside her, which is what he's after. Children do the same thing. Abusers are generally emotionally retarded men.

These men also express their insatiable need to control the women in their lives by trying to keep them constantly off balance. They ask her to do something, then change their minds at the last minute. A man may call home and surprise the woman with an announcement that turns her day upside down. Dr. Miller writes that a woman told her that her husband did this because "he likes to surprise me at the last minute." Dr. Miller corrected her, pointing out that "surprise," in this case, means "control."

We've mentioned that women being nonphysically abused stay trapped for a long time, because they're able to deny that what is happening to them is abuse. Dr. Miller writes:

> At first she has easy explanations and rationales for his behavior. If he becomes jealous, it's that he finds her desirable; she is flattered. If he insists on making all the decisions, it's that he wants to protect and shelter her; she feels cared for. If he won't communicate, it's that he is the strong silent type; she understands. If he embarrasses her or calls her names, it's that he just lost his temper and didn't mean it; she forgives. By the time she realizes he does mean it and she no longer feels flattered, cared for, or understanding—and certainly not forgiving—she finds herself in a relationship so skewed that she can't see a way out.

In other words, the woman tries to see the bright side in each situation. But she is deceiving herself. We have such a deep desire to keep peace in the family that we will tell ourselves the worst lies just so that we don't have to confront our partners with the truth. But this kind of lying extracts a phenomenal price: in the end, it emotionally bankrupts the woman.

How does a woman bankrupt herself emotionally? In the face of this manipulative abuse, she numbs her feelings. She numbs her reactions. She numbs her desires. She numbs her needs. Little by little she short-circuits her entire emotional apparatus and sense of being. She becomes one of the walking dead. She doesn't live, she merely functions. She doesn't move forward in life and she tries not to fall backward. Her attitude to life is that it's just to be gotten through. Gone are the hope, the joy, and the sense of discovery that makes life meaningful and beautiful. Her life has lost all its colors, and she sees everything as if on a black-and-white TV screen—gray and flat.

When she grows more and more oblivious to the abuser's attacks, he will usually aim his abuse at someone else in the home. That usually means the kids. His abuse of their mother is, in itself, child abuse: 80 to 90 percent of the children in abusive homes know what is happening to their family. The man will verbally pulverize the kids, insulting and grossly humiliating them, to get to his wife. He'll make them break down and cry and beg him to stop. He knows that this will work on the woman's maternal feelings; he wants to turn those against her by making her feel powerless to protect her children, and thus like a complete failure as a mother, wife, and woman.

If there are no children around, the man will torture the woman's pets. Batterers have set on fire the tails of cats and dogs to hurt their wives, and to let them know that they're next. From torturing the household pets, he'll go on to do her direct physical harm. Remember: abuse doesn't go away on its own, it just escalates.

"Men have mocked the Ph.D. their wife is studying for," writes Dr. Miller, "clipped buds off the rosebushes she nurtures, cut up her favorite dress, smeared feces on the bedroom wall she just painted, slandered her parents. Anything that hurts. Any way to degrade her." Her self-respect and self-confidence are amputated. Her sense of self is amputated. It's all done with no bloodshed, no bruises, and no broken bones. Her soul is simply crucified.

The report card on police response to nonphysical abuse has been dismal; ignorance and mistaken attitudes prevail. Police departments are being educated as to why they can't just shrug off family abuse. The brightest and the best are quick to learn and are changing. What makes cops take notice, explains Dr. Miller, is "their own liability, realizing that if they fail to act on a battering charge and the woman is later injured or killed—as all too often has been the case—they will be held personally responsible." Cops need to be educated on how to recognize and properly process the crime of abuse, and be made aware of the consequences of ignoring it.

Police attitudes are not improved by the fact that many policemen beat their wives. How bad is it? According to Dr. Miller, "64 percent of police officers have family violence." At a conference with forty-three police chiefs, a woman district attorney was explaining the need for a county domestic violence unit; after her closing statement, one of the police chiefs present said: "There isn't a guy in this room who doesn't think it's okay to beat your wife."

When a police officer's wife or girlfriend reports being abused, the majority of police departments turn a deaf ear and a blind eye. Female police officers have shown to be even worse than their male counterparts. Having been harassed and excluded during their training, they often make up their minds to "be men" as a means of self-defense. This leads them to copy, even exaggerate, what their male counterparts do. Whether male or female, police too often fail to protect abused women.

Are there signs of change? "To assure greater justice," writes Dr. Miller, "many communities have instituted arrest policies. The most effective is *a mandatory arrest policy that requires police to make an arrest in all family abuse calls;* similar to it is a pro-arrest policy that, while not requiring automatic arrest, urges it in most cases."

Further positive changes will come about in a couple of ways. Intelligent cops will educate themselves or be educated by their municipalities on why they can't continue with outdated attitudes. They'll get past their ignorance and stereotypes and learn the truth about abuse. Community programs are also noteworthy. One, in Quincy, Massachusetts, is called simply the Model Domestic Abuse Program. It has four goals, according to its manual:

1. *to protect and empower women who seek legal assistance*

2. *to encourage battered women to seek legal assistance*

3. *to control batterers and hold them accountable for their abuse*

4. *to prevent domestic abuse by redefining it as a serious crime in the minds of the public and the criminal justice community*

The Quincy program assumes that abuse can be stopped or prevented by the criminal justice system. To this end it coordinates the work of several agencies. Social services agencies work with all the divisions of the criminal justice system to make sure that they communicate with each other. The Quincy program works with the police department, providing extensive training, helping establish detailed policies and procedures. Arrest is mandatory, with a woman's safety as the primary concern, and there is careful follow-up. It brings in the district attorney's office, with lawyers and counselors ready to inform and support the woman throughout the court procedure. Finally, the court system is brought into the process. Abuse victims have a separate waiting room and are helped by an all-female staff; in addition, abuse cases have priority over nonabuse cases.

Another program, the Duluth (Minnesota) Domestic Abuse Intervention Project, began in the early 1980s and has been used as a model program by other cities. Currently, efforts are under way to try to adopt a version of it throughout New York State. The Duluth program provides seminars and training materials for shelter advocates, police officers, prosecutors, probation officers, judges, counselors, group facilitators, social services providers, and Native American service providers.

While these programs are just the beginning of the effort to deal with domestic violence, we must remember that they still primarily address *physical* abuse, not nonphysical abuse. Programs designed to help police identify abuse that shows no visible wounds are still to be developed.

Our courts treat abused women very badly. Would you believe it if we told you that some judges will sign decisions without ever seeing the woman or even reading the papers she filed? Unless you have experience with our legal system, you may have some naïve expectations and you may be in for a rude awakening. Dr. Miller writes:

> *Just as a woman's abusive partner turned her into a nonperson,*
> *so the court continues to treat her. . . . More than once I have*
> *seen judges read off the accusations on the petition before them*
> *only to discover from the court clerk's whisper that they have*
> *the wrong person. Often the judge rattles off his decision so rou-*

tinely and dismisses the woman so quickly that she leaves like a sleepwalker, not sure what has happened. "I don't think he even saw me," one woman said, looking back from the hall at the closed door of the courtroom.

This may give you a sense of where our courts and judges are on the abuse issue generally. "Judges have no special training in domestic violence," writes Dr. Miller, "but bring to the bench the same myths and misunderstandings all of us have; the rest they learn on the job. Many judges, having little knowledge of psychology, misinterpret a woman's responses to abuse. If she drops the charges against her mate instead of following through, the judge may condemn and castigate her like a naughty child. . . . If she hangs on to an abusive relationship for longer than the judge deems sensible, he or she may accuse her of stupidity." And the majority of judges are reluctant to order the batterers to vacate the homes they share with the wives they batter.

What's wrong with our judges? Just because they wear a black robe, sit on an elevated platform, and are called "Your Honor," they're not necessarily any less naïve or simpleminded than other people regarding domestic violence. Their perspective has been conditioned by the times and the beliefs of the culture in which they matured.

What happens when a woman goes to court? First, she'll be asked to wait, possibly for hours, in a crowded room with wooden benches. In that same room will be men called to appear in court; some of them may have to be quieted down or removed by the court officers. There will also be fidgety children increasing the tension in the room. When the woman's name is called, she will be escorted into the courtroom by a police officer. Inside the courtroom, she will stand alone in front of the judge, the court reporter, the court clerk, and the court police officer with his revolver in plain view. Not uncommonly, none of these four people will even look at her during the entire process; that's how dehumanized and emotionally sterile it can be. Each participant will contribute his bit in a completely mechanical fashion. The judge will state his decision, and that will be that. The whole thing is cold, frightening, and embarrassing, nothing less than social abuse.

Of course, if a man other than a woman's husband or boyfriend were to do to her what a batterer does, the whole criminal justice system would jump to her rescue. Consider these four acts below that are part of what a criminal court will prosecute. "If anyone other than an abusive husband committed these four acts," writes Dr. Miller, "and anyone but an abused wife reported them, they would surely warrant fines or arrests." They are acts of wife battering:

- *disorderly conduct:* yelling, obscenity, name calling, breaking windows, kicking in doors

- *harassment:* following her, hiding her keys, letting air out of the tires of her car, not allowing visits with family or friends, phoning her repeatedly, breaking her favorite things, disparaging her, making unreasonable demands

- *menacing in the third degree:* locking her in a closet, locking her out of the house, waving a weapon before her, hitting her pet, cutting up her clothes, pretending to punch her

- *reckless endangerment:* driving a child without a seat belt; forcing the woman out of the house at night, not letting her take prescribed medication, forcing her to drink or take drugs

These are all acts of nonphysical abuse; the family court system still hasn't caught on that women deserve to be protected from them.

Finally, what attitude do women in our society have toward non-physical violence? Women who have never experienced abuse seem to divide into two groups: those who hate the abuser and those who hate the abused. You might imagine that all women are appalled by the idea that millions of women suffer physical violence and nonphysical abuse, but that's not the case. The women who want to put away the batterers and throw away the key do everything they can to try to educate the public. The other group, of women who hate battered women, is surprisingly large. Their attitude can do abused women great harm.

Such women argue that we are all responsible for our actions. They insist that if a woman stays in an abusive situation she deserves what she gets: why doesn't she just get out, rather than sitting there and getting the hell beaten out of her? Some will even go so far as to argue that to focus on battered women helps keep women thinking that they can't take charge of their lives. Our argument that abusive men brainwash their women, they say, encourages women to think that they can't help themselves. Women hostile to our views may insist that women can help themselves if they stop listening to "rhetoric" that characterizes them as victims, helpless, brainwashed, and trapped.

Why would women take this view? First of all, those who have not been in an abusive relationship have no direct knowledge of what it feels like or how they would respond if they became victims. Unless someone tells them about it or they read about it, they have no way of knowing the fear and despair that grip the souls of battered women.

Also, women who feel contempt for battered women may be trying to fit in with the male establishment: "Your enemy is my enemy." But this is crazy thinking: can any woman ever truly join a male establishment that puts women down? Further, certain women attack victims of abuse to try to distance themselves from something they hate within themselves and see glaring at them in battered women: their position of weakness and submission. Dr. Mary Miller writes: "According to psychiatrists, these women are using the defense mechanism of projection. Since it hurts to be cast by society in an inferior role, they unload the powerlessness they feel onto abused women to avoid feeling it themselves."

One final reason some women despise abuse victims is the tendency we all have to scapegoat. When we don't want to take responsibility—even if we keep saying that we must take responsibility—we just blame others. These women are simply blaming others who, they say, blame others for the misery in their lives. It's ironic.

Nonphysical abuse leads the women who are its victims to believe that they can't do anything right. They feel that they are going crazy but that they can't tell anyone because *there are no visible wounds.* The victim of nonphysical abuse will experience isolation and a deep longing to get back in touch with relatives and friends. But money is usually an issue: abused women are always penniless. The attitude of police, until recently, has been that this is just another domestic dispute and not a crime. The courts' response has been, "Please go home and work it out by yourselves." And a surprising number of women who have never been abused reject the testimony of battered women.

The good news is that more information is emerging on this subject than ever before. Slowly, attitudes are being changed. Slowly, more and more Americans are becoming knowledgeable and therefore enlightened about this, the darkest of America's secrets.

Chapter 7

Is There a Cure for These Men?

If you are a man reading this book, you may have identified directly with some of our descriptions of the batterer; if you're a woman, you may finally have found an explanation for what has been wrong in your marriage or relationship for years. Once you get over the initial shock of such a realization, a question arises: Can a batterer be cured? Having asked that question, we want to make it absolutely clear right away that *this chapter is not meant to help you justify staying in an abusive relationship.* Too many women stay too long in battering relationships because of the false hope that their abuser will change into the loving man he seems to be during the honeymoon phase of the cycle of violence. *Don't stay.* Separate from him first, and see if he will take the steps he must take to get well.

To the men who have read this far and have recognized in these pages their own behavior, I would first like to say that reading this kind of book is a big step. Many batterers are so twisted that they will not admit that they have this problem. Not being able to see it, they stay stuck. Others may recognize their behavior and feelings in these pages, but don't want to deal squarely with the problem. If you've recognized yourself in these pages and do truly want to change, then you're already a lot further along than many others. I would say to you that, whether or not you've ever been in any kind of therapy, *the best thing you can do for yourself is to get into a therapy program right away.*

What you're looking for is group therapy that focuses on anger and battering. Doing this will give you a new lease on life. Change won't happen overnight. You're definitely going to be put through some hard times, and *the work does require courage.* The question you want to ask yourself is: what's the payoff? What you'll get is a whole new sense of self-control. You will discover new things about yourself. You'll see what sets you off, producing the actions and moods that wreck your life. You will come into a new knowledge that will help you master yourself. That's called self-knowledge. And you'll discover a whole new way to relate to women, which will open up a new range of good experiences you can't even dream about right now. Most of all, the work of therapy will free you from a life that's empty, hopeless, and full of shame and guilt.

Before you start calling around to find a group, you also need to know that there are some groups you should avoid. The first type includes the so-called men's movement groups: they're big on men expressing their anger toward women—and trust us, that's not the kind of group that will help you. You need the exact opposite: to learn to relate to women in a way that will bring happiness into your life and hers. You don't need to learn new reasons to be angry with women. Not all "men's movement" groups are for men who hate women, but do be aware that such groups are out there.

Also avoid the "feminist men" groups, because instead of getting you to talk about your experience as a man, these groups will try to convince you that men and women shouldn't talk about their differences. Such a group will not provide a place where you can understand your feelings, because their members tend to believe they shouldn't discuss anger toward partners.

To sum up, you don't want to get into any group that takes either extreme attitude—"Let's rage against women" or "Let's not bring up anger at all." Look for a group with minimal ideology, a group where men come to talk honestly because they're tired of lying and they want to breathe some truth back into their lives. The leader just helps to steer and focus discussion, without forcing the group to buy into a particular interpretation. Remember, you're looking for some truth.

At your first meeting, don't be in any hurry to spill your guts to everyone. Go in, sit down, get familiar with all the faces in the room. You don't have to say anything you don't want to say. You may not feel comfortable at first, so say nothing, just listen. There's nothing wrong with letting others talk about what they're going through. Pick your time when you're going to speak, and make the commitment to yourself that you're not going to lie. If you feel that you can't trust the group, say so. At the same time, when you say something, speak the truth. You can keep on lying outside the meeting, but in the meeting tell the truth. And remember, you want to be able to say what's on your mind without getting shot down. If you do get shot down, join another group.

How can you find a good therapy group? Dr. Donald Dutton suggests calling the local United Way chapter. The United Way organization has a family services group that focuses on anger management. Call churches, synagogues, mosques, court services, and civic health programs. Also, call some therapists and see if you can find two or three who specialize in anger management. Go to each for an initial visit, and after you've met them all, pick one. If you can afford it, see that person at least once a week besides going to group. Dr. Dutton believes that groups are generally the better choice, because of the support members offer one another. But both, if you can afford it, are the ideal.

In the beginning, it is normal to be a little nervous and ashamed. But don't let these feelings stop you. Attend a group for four months and see what you can learn about yourself.

In *The Batterer*, Dr. Dutton discusses what men can do to find healing, and why they're reluctant to start treatment. First, a man may fear losing the woman and finding himself alone. Second, he's likely to be reluctant to open up to other men. All of us hesitate to drag out our dirty laundry in front of people we hardly know. But the third and most important reason men stay away from these groups is the fear of having to face something deep inside themselves that is too horrible for them to handle. We're talking about deeply buried fear and shame. (This point is illustrated beautifully in the movie *The Prince of Tides*, with Barbra Streisand and Nick Nolte. In the movie, a family secret results in deaths and suicide attempts. Finally, when the secret is discussed, healing comes; people are transformed by having spoken the truth.)

Dr. Dutton describes a typical group, giving many details and a good explanation of what happens. Before being accepted in the group, the participants have been screened; the therapist who heads the group interviewed them. On "Opening Night"—the first time the group meets—the men go around the circle and talk about their past therapy experience. Some question the qualifications of the therapist; others explain why their past therapy failed: "It was the therapist's fault!" Eventually, the conversation turns to why they are there. One or two men will talk openly about how they battered their wife or girlfriend. The others listen and identify. The group gets focused and some truth comes out. Therapists who head these groups can usually tell when the participants are being honest.

Is the truth-telling like confession in church? Essentially, therapy *is* a type of confession. As some speak the truth, they are released from what these lies have been doing in their lives. Others in the group are helped simply by hearing what these other men have done. Those listening hear other men admit things they themselves haven't wanted to talk about, and they face their own shame as others express theirs openly.

Therapy groups usually have some ground rules. For instance, members have to come on time, remain sober and drug-free, not discuss outside the group what is talked about during sessions, and speak the truth. Also, from the start the basic idea is that if you batter someone, the violence is your responsibility. Nobody else is to blame. The two big problems therapists face in these groups are getting the men to admit and recognize that they are batterers, and teaching them to take responsibility for their actions.

What's the most important thing a group like this tries to teach the men who participate? In simple terms: if you beat up on somebody it's your fault, not the fault of the person you beat up. Battering men have had a lifetime of blaming others, and this is why it's so hard to drill into their conscience the idea that their violence is *their* violence. Healing starts the moment a man accepts responsibility for his actions. The ones who do well and recover are the ones able to face themselves and accept the truth that they are batterers.

Some group therapists will have each man sign a contract stating clearly that if he acts violent in any way, the violence is his fault. This usually angers the men; some just storm out of the meeting, only to return apologetically next time. Batterers in group therapy will try every con game imaginable with the therapist, but therapists who work with batterers are usually familiar with every lie out there. There is nothing new under the sun. And the therapist will explain at the onset that these sessions will challenge and confront participants, even "get in their face." The men are taught that there's a difference between the confrontation that takes place in the group and the kind of attacks they've experienced in life. Confrontation in the group is not designed to abuse the person, but instead to make him face things inside himself that he wouldn't acknowledge otherwise. That will makes him stronger, more in control of himself, because it sets him free from things he's hidden from himself. Speak the truth and you are set free.

Batterers' therapy groups teach the men new tools and new skills, which equip them with powerful new ways to change their own lives. The new tools and skills involve learning how to separate what these men fight about with their partners (money, sex, drugs) from all the emotions that surge when these subjects come up. Then they learn to look at the feelings. Next, they are taught to talk about feelings such as fear, shame, humiliation, and grief. By identifying these emotions and learning when they come into play, the men learn to see how their anger is just a cover-up for them. Fear, shame, humiliation, and grief trigger feelings of shame, stupidity, vulnerability, and weakness; a man who feels them may think of himself as less than a man. In order to deny such feelings, he flies into a rage and beats up his partner. The anger is just a way of denying other feelings.

Therapy groups use role-playing exercises, in which the men act out scenes that at home would lead up to violence. In a controlled situation, they learn to identify points where they could simply have stopped and not gone any further. In learning this, they are also learning to acquire a new kind of control: self-control. The men learn that if they can keep a situation from exploding, calm down, and bring the problem to a peaceful resolution, they will achieve a new kind of power in their lives.

The therapist will lead his group into clearly defining acts of physical, sexual, and verbal abuse against people, things, and pets, and explain that falling into abuse is like falling into an addiction. Abuse may not seem like alcohol or drugs, but batterers are abuse junkies, addicted to violence. In a therapy group the men are asked: Did you ever do such and such to your wife or girlfriend? Did you

ever do something like it but a little different? Have you ever noticed that you do this in all your relationships with women?

Another difficult hurdle for abusive men is learning not to scapegoat their partner, not to blame her. This issue carries a lot of
shame, so the therapist won't bring it up too soon, or the men will
just clam up. Timing is crucial.

After the group has met for three or four weeks, the therapist
may give the members a questionnaire dealing with childhood and
family. Men became batterers in large part because of their childhoods, so asking them to write about childhood is certain to dredge
up a lot of shame, embarrassment, anger, humiliation, and grief.
Consequently, the questionnaire usually isn't well received. The
men will be asked to take it home to fill out, and to bring it back
at the next session. Typically they'll bring it back to the therapist
four or five sessions later.

As the group continues, its members will be taught more techniques for coping with rage. They'll write out the story of their last
act of battering or episode of anger, and they'll keep a journal of every
act of anger or violence. As they narrate what happened, they learn
to take apart the event like an auto mechanic taking apart a car engine. First they identify the trigger, what set them off in the first
place. What did she say? What did he say? Next they rate the event
on a scale of 1 to 10 (for example, 1 being loud words and 10 being
violence serious enough to send the victim to the hospital). Third,
they study and learn to recognize all the ingredients that came together before the violence occurred: What were they talking about
before he got angry? What did he start thinking at the beginning of
the episode? What kind of verbal insults did he use as he built up
his anger? Finally, what thoughts, words, and actions did he use to
calm himself down and control the situation? Men learn a lot about
themselves through these exercises, and through them can gain
mastery over the rage that has been controlling them all their lives.

In the later stage of the group, the men begin to exchange phone numbers and to help each other outside group meetings. They get to know each other well enough to spot lies and confront each other with them.

Typically, the deepest work done in the group comes when the discussion turns toward early childhood and the men's parents. The men have to talk about how the parents related to each other and to the kids. As we mentioned earlier, this is deeply painful work. But by doing it, the men can discover where their internal triggers are. It is precisely these triggers that have to be rewired—or removed altogether—so the men can live free from the desire to batter. This is what the therapy process is about.

Much of the talk concerns how these men were victimized and what roles both parents played. One especially enraging subject is often the mother's having had a lover. As for the father, he usually shamed the son and tried to hammer into him that he was no good and would never amount to anything. To hear this over and over again, year after year, shapes a child's entire outlook. Instead of getting what he needs—confidence, trust, love, support—he's poisoned with the exact opposite.

These open confessions truly cement the group. During them, the men's worst suffering is brought out into the open. One great difficulty participants in a treatment program have when it ends is going back to superficial conversation. They have tasted the deepest kind of conversation and confession. They will often stay close to members of the group, or they may return to their previous isolation.

Is psychotherapy the cure for domestic violence? If not, then what other help is available for batterers? How do we stop domestic violence in America?

Even the best programs report that 40 to 60 percent of the men they treat return to abusive behavior within five years. Most experts agree that the best program in existence is the Domestic Abuse Intervention Project in Duluth, Minnesota, whose figures these are. Fully half the men treated for battering go back to battering. So psychotherapy alone is not the answer. It is one of the answers. What are the others?

Looking at how this country has dealt with other kinds of destructive behavior, we get valuable lessons. Two examples: smoking, which kills tens of thousands every year, and drunk driving, which kills thousands of innocent people yearly on the road. As a nation, we have tackled these two kinds of destructive behaviors, and they offer us good models. We are confident that the United States can do the same for domestic violence.

In 1974, François was at a school board meeting in his hometown, Laguna Beach, California. The head of a philanthropic foundation arranged to have two professors from the University of California–Irvine medical school address the board on the subject of eliminating smoking at board meetings. The philanthropist believed that smoking was a health hazard and that the school board could set an example for students by not smoking. The two professors were nationally recognized experts. They made an excellent presentation. The president of the school board was a doctor. The school board turned them down. Twenty years later, everyone's attitude has changed, even though some of the wealthiest companies in America promote smoking with some of the best lobbying money can buy. The American Cancer Society spent millions of dollars to educate the public through media campaigns and literature for schools. The truth has prevailed.

Another deadly behavior that was fashionable or at least culturally accepted: drinking and driving. Like smoking, drunk driving was everywhere, in the movies, and on television. It was tolerated, even encouraged by some advertising. The work that changed this attitude included a mass education campaign spearheaded by Mothers Against Drunk Driving. MADD generated income to develop a nationwide media campaign. As a result, driving under the influence is now punished more rigorously, and the phrase "designated driver" has become part of everyone's vocabulary.

The first step toward ending domestic violence, therefore, involves education. We must educate adults so that they no longer ask questions such as "Why do battered women stay in these relationships?" We must also educate children before they develop negative attitudes toward women. Our kids need to learn that men and women are equal and that the need for control leads to abuse.

Next, it is vital for everyone to understand why men batter. We need to become aware of all the excuses that have helped men avoid taking responsibility for their actions. Most abused women testify that their husbands explain away their violent acts, saying things like "I just lose it"; "It's her fault, she made me do it"; or (the favorite) "Men have always beaten their wives. How else are they gonna learn anything?" Other men blame their behavior on drugs or alcohol. The truth is that abusive men have twisted minds even before they enter the abusive relationship. Their violence is a learned behavior, and it can be unlearned.

We need education, but that alone is not enough. A second step toward ending domestic violence is reform of our legal system, which too often treats the battered woman so badly that she feels it has picked up where the batterer left off. Our legal system has only recently begun to address the battered-woman syndrome, to understand why battered women do not have the options people commonly assume they have. As we've explained, a battered woman can't leave, because she can't even think for herself. She has lost that capacity because she has been tortured and brainwashed. Since her thinking is largely impaired, how can we expect her to make the rational and sane choices that a nonabused person can make? Furthermore, it's not safe for her to leave. And she's not capable of thinking of divorce; that's like thinking of suicide, in her circumstances. Our legal system still fails to understand much of this, and women face problems at every step of the way out.

(It is tragic that the way most American law students learn about domestic violence is by studying court cases in which the accused is a battered woman who has killed her husband. The truth is, most victims of domestic violence are women. *That* is the lesson that should be taught in our law schools.)

A couple of programs we mentioned earlier, one in Quincy, Massachusetts, and the other in Duluth, Minnesota, are bright spots. They work because they bring together the efforts of the social services agencies with those of all the divisions of the criminal justice system and require continual communication among them. The police receive extensive training on how to handle domestic violence; there are detailed procedures; arrest is mandatory, with the woman's safety being the primary concern; and cases are systematically followed up. The Quincy and Duluth programs bring in the district attorney's office, with specially trained lawyers and counselors to help the woman throughout the courtroom procedure and afterward. The courts give priority to scheduling abuse cases. After the woman is given a protective order, the batterer is put under surveillance by the probation department. Officers monitor the man's behavior, establishing and maintaining contact with his friends, his relatives, and the agencies that deal with him. The batterer is required to participate actively in a treatment program such as we described above. Unlike most group therapy programs, this one keeps in close contact with the abuser's mate and with the police, probation officer, and court should the abuser show signs that he intends to commit further abuse.

This approach has been used in San Diego, California, with

stunning success: the city's domestic violence homicide rate has dropped 60 percent. *Education saves lives.*

So is there a cure for violent men? We do not have 100 percent success with any single approach. Our entire culture has to change its attitudes toward domestic violence. Each person can begin to learn enough about it to at least dispel the myths we all seem to believe. This means you: learn, and teach others what you are learning. We can become informed advocates for change. It will require a small effort by many Americans, and the goal is pure: to save lives that are being destroyed.

Chapter 8

What About Going to a Church
or Temple for Counseling?

Battered women who've received counseling from the clergy often say that when they left the pastor, rabbi, mullah, or priest, they felt worse than when they arrived. Why is that? What did their clergyperson say to make them feel this way? How should women approach counseling from the clergy?

Being a pastor, I find it painful to admit that church ministers don't always know what to tell victims of domestic violence. In this chapter, I am going to speak to you as a Christian pastor, but I believe that this is also true of Judaism and Islam. And I would be surprised if it didn't apply to other faiths as well. An excellent resource for Jewish readers is *The Shame Borne in Silence: Spouse Abuse in the Jewish Community*, by Rabbi Abraham Twerski, M.D.

Life's issues are complex; the Bible answers some issues clearly and others not so clearly. My point is simply this: if you are a woman being battered and you go to your clergy for counseling, recognize that you are dealing with men and women who are imperfect, sinners just like you, and they can give you wrong counseling. In fact, unless they have studied domestic violence, they probably don't know very much about it.

So don't think that every word out of a pastor's mouth is God's counsel. The Bible teaches that we should seek more than one counselor, and that in a group of counselors there is wisdom. Your pastor can pray with you, and you can ask him or her for a referral—either to a Christian therapist who specializes in domestic abuse or to community resources. If the pastor doesn't have any referrals to give you, *find your own.* When you are in recovery from your abuse, go back and share with him what you found. Insist that he read this book.

If you go to a clergyperson for counseling, interview him before you discuss your circumstances. Ask about his counseling experience. Has he taken courses in psychology at a college or university? Does he believe that psychological principles can be combined with biblical principles? If a minister gives you the impression that psychology and the Bible cannot go together, you might want to excuse yourself and leave. This person is a Bible teacher, not the kind of counselor you are looking for. He may be good to go and see when you have questions about what the Bible says.

If you find yourself talking with such a person, you have just encountered one of the main problems in our clergy. There are priests and pastors who will offer to counsel you but have no background in psychology. Worse, they may even oppose all forms of psychology, believing that it is from the devil.

The word *counselor* is just now being more clearly defined in the church, as more pastors and priests receive training to do psychological counseling. A distinction is being made between *emotional* counseling and *pastoral* counseling: the first is psychological counseling that focuses on a person's emotional well-being, and the second is spiritual counseling that focuses on interpreting the Bible so as to help a person grow spiritually.

Remember, the person writing this is a pastor. I am not criticizing the church or Christianity, Judaism, or Islam. I want to warn you against some attitudes that are often accepted by the clergy but that are wrong and contrary to the message of the Bible. That is another problem within the church: church people and church counselors may interpret the Bible mistakenly.

So what is the one thing you want to look out for as a woman? It's this: when speaking with a pastor or a priest, find out how he understands the role of women in life and in the church. Does he see woman as "the weaker vessel"? The Bible calls a man's wife the weaker vessel (1 Peter 3:7). Some men, taking that concept out of context, think of women as less than men. The Bible is not anti-woman. Stupid men are anti-woman, and they twist what the Bible says. They are closely followed by groups of otherwise brilliant women who, in this case, have an ax to grind, and therefore likewise twist what the Bible says. An anti-woman man will claim that the Bible says women are less smart than men, less rational, less reliable, not as strong spiritually, emotionally, or physically. The Bible says nothing of the kind.

The actual verse says: "Husbands, likewise dwell with [your wives] with understanding, giving honor to the wife, as to the weaker vessel, and as being heirs together of the grace of life, that your prayers may not be hindered." There is great beauty in this verse. The relationship it describes between the husband and the wife exemplifies a profound love between a man and a woman. The verse elevates both spouses when it speaks of them as being "heirs together of the grace of life." In other words, their lives are not just empty, futile, and meaningless, but rather have great meaning in the eyes of God. In that context, the "weaker vessel" is never put down or abused, but protected and cared for.

This is Christianity under the best conditions, and this is not the world that most Christians live in. The very last thing this passage says is that women are less than men, although, unfortunately, that is how many men in the church see it. Why do these men do this? Because we are all imperfect, selfish, and self-serving; we see what we want to see and hear what we want to hear. God is perfecting us. We're simply not there yet.

The Bible uses the word *submit* in connection with what women are to do in their marriages. This is another example of a word taken out of context and twisted in its meaning; you can be sure that the wrong, self-serving interpretation is widespread in the church. To my mind, *submit* is one of the most misused and abused of all words. Where does it appear in the Bible? This is the passage; please read it all the way through and then go back and consider what *submit* means:

> *Wives, submit to your own husbands, as to the Lord. For the husband is head of the wife, as also Christ is head of the church; and He is the Savior of the body. Therefore, just as the church is subject to Christ, so let the wives be to their own husbands in everything. Husbands, love your wives, just as Christ also loved the church and gave Himself for it, that He might sanctify and cleanse it with the washing of water by the word, that He might present it to Himself a glorious church, not having spot or wrinkle or any such thing, but that it should be holy and without blemish. So husbands ought to love their own wives as their own bodies; he who loves his wife loves himself.*
> (Ephesians 5:22–28 [New King James Version])

First, the obvious: you will note that this passage does not tell women to submit to their men like an animal or a doormat. *Women are equated here with the highest work of God—the church.* By "the church," we don't mean the building where you go to worship. We mean the spiritual entity made up of people all over the world, in all denominations and nondenominations, who love God and are deeply thankful for what Jesus has done for us. *Submission here is with joy and gladness, not out of fear or ritualistic duty.* But if you take the first verse out of context, thereby twisting the meaning and lying about what it says, and just tell women—as I have heard batterers do—"The Bible says you are to submit," and if you say this often enough, then people will begin to believe the false interpretation. Don't be fooled. Also, don't condemn the Bible as chauvinistic or anti-woman because of the attitudes of some of the men in church.

Such attitudes can lead these men to make the worst possible mistake when they counsel you. What is that mistake? A counselor who misinterprets the Bible can leave you feeling that you, the victim, are somehow the cause of all the abuse that is happening to you. In other words, with no training in psychological issues they may completely misread what's really going on in your life. If they don't understand the problem, they will not be able to give you the right answers. Also, they may think that since you are the "weaker vessel," what you think or have to say is simply not as significant as what your husband has to say. And finally, the idea that you are to "submit" may have led them to believe that a woman who has any problem with her man must be at fault—if she just submitted, everything would be well, the family would live happily, there would be world peace. The trouble with the world, according to this attitude, is that women are rebellious.

What do battered women think of church counseling? I can only share with you what some women have told me. They have walked away with the uncomfortable feeling that they've been told, though not in so many words, that they were the cause of the bad marriage or the abuse. In other words, they walked in as victims hoping to find relief and help, and walked away feeling worse—feeling beaten and victimized again. Though not all women have this experience, most of the women I have talked with did.

You'll remember that earlier in this book we talked about how our society has all kinds of misconceptions about domestic violence. Our churches share those attitudes. We wrote that people can't believe respectable men could do such things to their wives, and we talked about financial and emotional pressures that keep women in abusive relationships. Most pastors and ministers simply don't know much about these things. They may have heard something; they may have read an article or two. But mostly, this knowledge is new and hasn't yet caught on widely.

What other counseling tips do pastors and priests give women that may make things worse for them? The Bible teaches that we must forgive. It says that we must love our enemy even if he acts unkindly. It teaches that a wife must submit to the direction of her husband. It teaches that the virtuous woman provides for her family. It teaches that a woman needs to put her marriage in God's hands, and God will change the man.

When a pastor says these things to a battered woman, what's her response going to be? She is thinking that she doesn't feel forgiveness toward her batterer. She doesn't feel love for this man who's beating her physically, nonphysically, or both. She has probably wished him dead many times. Thanks to the counseling session she will feel that this is the worst sin imaginable. She'll believe that she is sinning in all these areas. She takes this idea further: surely God can't forgive a woman who secretly wishes her husband dead. She's a horrible sinner and God can't possibly love her. Maybe her father abused her or her mother; she overlays that experience on her concept of God and sees Him as angry with her. By the time she leaves that counseling session, she feels that everything is her fault.

Did the pastor say anything wrong? Not really. Did he say anything right? Not really. Did he understand the victim and how she felt? Probably not. He told her what the Bible says *in general*.

What does the Bible say about a man who beats his wife? The husband is to love his wife, treat her with dignity, strengthen her, care for her. He is to love her as Jesus loves the church. Do you see Jesus battering and violating the church? Jesus died for the church. Jesus does not condemn the church or any of its members.

He pours out His forgiveness, patience, and sacrificial love upon the church.

What does the Bible say about instilling fear in a woman through physical or psychological abuse? If a man uses fear to control his wife, this is a sin. The Bible teaches that pure love casts out all fear (1 John 4:18). Whenever a man demands, commands, orders, or in any way makes a woman fearful, he is in sin. He opposes God.

What does the Bible teach us to do if someone sins against us? In the Gospel of Matthew, chapter 18, we are given a procedure:

> *Moreover if your brother sins against you, go and tell him his fault between you and him alone. If he hears you, you have gained your brother. But if he will not hear you, take with you one or two more, that "by the mouth of two or three witnesses every word may be established." And if he refuses to hear them, tell it to the church. But if he refuses even to hear the church, let him be to you like a heathen and a tax collector* (Matthew 18:15–17).

Will this procedure work with a batterer? Unfortunately, the answer is usually no. If a woman is being abused by her husband physically or psychologically, telling him his fault will probably only make things worse, once the person who told him his fault has left.

What good, then, is this passage? The Bible teaches that if the sinner will not hear you, will not listen to you and another person, and will reject what the church has to say, then you are to *treat him like a nonbeliever.* The church stands on what the Bible says. If he is physically or nonphysically abusive, the Bible tells you that he is not in the will of God.

The Bible teaches what the responsibilities of the husband are in Ephesians 5.

There is a passage in the New Testament where a man is beating, not his wife, but his servants. Needless to say, in the eyes of God a wife is more important in a man's life than a servant. In a parable (Luke 12:45–46), Jesus describes a man who is beating his servants and thinks that he can get away with it because his own master is not around. In the next verse Jesus says that when this batterer's master returns, the batterer will be sorely punished and be treated as a nonbeliever. Jesus ends by saying, "To whom much is given, from him much will be required." In other words, a husband is to consider his wife a great gift from God, which means that *if he mistreats her in the smallest of ways, he is mistreating what God has given him.* She is not his personal property or a toy to play with. The Bible teaches that a wife is the most precious of gifts that a man can receive from God, and if the man harms her in any way, the man rejects God, God's teachings and principles, and God's love.

As we mentioned, in both the passage from Matthew and the parable in Luke, Jesus says that those who continue in these sins are like heathens or nonbelievers. So a battered woman is to look upon her abusive husband as a non-Christian or a nonbeliever. A man can say that he is a Christian and that he believes in Jesus, but if he beats his wife or torments her, he is out of line with the basic teaching of the Bible. Jesus teaches that on the day of judgment many will call out to Him and say that they did all kinds of things in his name; He will respond, "I never knew you." Anybody can say he's a Christian; it's what we do that establishes who we are.

Can a woman being battered by her husband receive the blessings of God for leaving the relationship? Many batterers will commit adultery, and when that happens, God blesses the separation. But what if he doesn't commit adultery? Remember: if he batters you or frightens you, he is sinning against what God calls him to do. *Depart from him* and wait to see if he will change (1 Corinthians 7:11).

And do not go back to him unless you are sure that he has changed. The proof will be in his actions, not simply in what he says to you. Abusive men always have a good verbal game going. As mentioned above, Jesus teaches that you will know people not by what they say, but by what they do. Any man can say that he will change. What program or group therapy did he go to that brought about the change? Did he work with a therapist for six months or a year? A pattern of abusive behavior is very hard to change. Battered women's shelters run by devout Christians have a firm rule that the woman should see six full months of excellent behavior, plus regular attendance at therapy and payment of support to her and the children, before she starts therapy with him or reconciles with him.

What should you hear from a pastor or a priest who is counseling you correctly? He should be able to tell you if he has training in psychology or some special ministry experience that qualifies him to help you. He may be especially gifted by God, so that he can help you even if he has no degree in psychology; on the other hand, just because he has studied psychology, it doesn't follow that he knows it all. At least, though, he should not be antipsychology.

You should have a sense that this counselor is *gifted in listening*. Watch him as he listens to you. Is he really listening or is he quick to try to fix your problem? Gifted counselors know that *listening is far more important than giving a quick solution*, because listening is an important healing act.

Finally, do you walk away feeling that this man truly *believed you and believed in you?* If not, the problem is not with you. Look around until you find someone able to truly minister to you.

If the issue is psychological, as we implied above, why even go to a church? The issues a battered woman faces are not just psychological. Certainly, you have been deeply damaged emotionally, and you need help on that level right away. If someone is physically hurt and bleeding and needs to go to an emergency room, we take care of their body before we talk to them about God in their lives.

But it's also true that the sin of battering is designed to harm the soul of the woman. Healing her emotions is psychological work. Healing her innermost being, her spiritual trust in God, is deeper still; her soul is the core of her being.

That healing essentially involves one question: How does she perceive God now? Does she hate God for having allowed this to happen in her life? Does she feel that God will reject her because she feels this anger and hatred toward Him? For a woman who believes in God this is a crucial issue.

This spiritual restoration is a work of God—not just of well-intentioned friends and counselors, though God uses them, as well as everything else in life, to bring about His plan for your life. Spiritual restoration takes time and needs patience. At the heart of it is what a person believes about God, and as the healing proceeds, your heartfelt understanding of God will be far deeper and greater than it has ever been. Your suffering will have left behind the best possible spiritual fruits: love, patience, a nonjudgmental attitude, and a new depth of character. You will know directly how God takes the worst things in our lives and transforms them into the best.

One day, you will look back, sigh long and deep, and, with hindsight, know how and why all these calamities happened to you. Until that time, your most important spiritual need is simply to know God as a Person who dwells inside you and feels every moment of pain at the moment that you feel it. His spirit dwells within us, and He knows more intimately than we can ever realize every painful heartbeat, every tormented thought, and every crushing blow.

Why does He allow us to suffer? I don't have a good answer to that question right now. My belief is that one day I will. For now, I have to trust and believe, although I still can't see all of the reasons behind what is happening. That's what faith is. That's what the spiritual life is based upon.

—FRANÇOIS DUBAU

As a battered woman in 1988, I had real problems finding counseling in church; from what I hear, it's still pretty difficult out there. My batterer started attending church after I left him, and he was able to convince many church members that I was at fault for leaving him. He found support either by pretending to have converted to Christianity, or by telling everyone what a devoted father and husband he was. He was able to do what I had not been able to do: get support from others.

But that's not what church is for. Church is where we go for fellowship—not to get rich or to get admiration, but to worship God and learn about Him. It took me about seven years to get back to church after feeling I had been abandoned by the side of the road. Non-Christians and Christians alike tended to my wounds like the Good Samaritan of the New Testament. I knew I was not walking alone, but with God carrying me every step of the way.

I can't advise you to see a pastor for counseling about battering. I feel you need secular support from battered women's shelters. If they are demeaning to your faith, stand up for it in group sessions. You will probably find, instead, that there are many women like yourself who are searching for God's grace in a terrible situation. Pastors, in general, simply are not trained to deal with violence.

I know many Christian women refuse to go to non-Christians for help and counsel, but that is not biblical. Remember that the Good Samaritan (Luke 10:33) of the Bible was not a religious person, yet he helped the injured person abandoned by the roadside. The Good Samaritan was doing God's will. Test every counsel that comes your way. Listen and filter all of it, and look for supportive people and ideas. *If someone tells you you are the problem, don't listen.* You are beginning the journey to recovery by reading this. You may have already left the batterer. *People who don't understand the process simply cannot help you.*

If you do leave the batterer and want Scripture that will empower you to know that you are not sinning against the God who loves you, I suggest you read 1 Corinthians 7:15:

> *But if the unbeliever leaves, let him do so. A believing man or woman is not bound in such circumstances; God has called us to live in peace.*

I didn't even hear of this verse until just recently, but when I did, I felt an enormous burden lifted from my heart. I had been *abandoned through violence* long before I left my batterer. Even if your husband or boyfriend is a Christian, if he is violent, he's acting like a nonbeliever (and worse). He has abandoned you by violating his promise to God to behave as Christ called him to. "God has called us to live in peace." I never hear about Jesus doing anything violent, except maybe overturning the tables of the money changers at the Temple in Jerusalem. Even then, He was clearing His Father's house of robbers and thieves.

Be strong. Know that God does not want you to sit at home if your husband or the father of your children is hurting you. Step out in faith. Read the next section and know that *God, not your batterer, is the Lord.* I know how scared you feel and how you hope someone will hear your pain and understand your fears. God will. If your pastor won't—well, he's not God. He may, though, have some resources to refer you to. In California, where I live, there are some Christian shelters for battered women. But you don't have to go to a special shelter; you only have to find your way out of the painful, dangerous situation you are in. Or perhaps you are already physically safe and now need to find your way to healing. Either way, remember: no matter how much your religion may appear to keep you stuck in your violent relationship, only one spiritual force would want you to be hurt and suffering. And that's the same one that beguiled Eve into doing the wrong thing. The Lord God wants you to be loved and happy; He wants you to be a light in the darkness of this world. He wants you to be alive to share His truth with others. So don't let other people keep you in an unsafe situation. *God is love, and love will not abuse you.*

—MERRITT McKEON

Chapter 9

Who Speaks for Kids?

Moments after her father fatally shot her mother in the Los Angeles Civil Courts Building, a sobbing six-year-old girl told sheriff's deputies: "Mommy and Daddy were talking, and Mommy said something Daddy didn't like, so he shot her," a deputy testified. Harry Zelig then approached deputies standing by his dying wife and calmly said: "I'm here. I did it." Zelig, a Woodland Hills physician, shot his ex-wife, Eileen, forty, after a child support hearing. The Zeligs had fought a bitter divorce battle, and in court papers Eileen Zelig stated she feared that her husband wanted to harm her.[1]

Domestic violence thrives on ignorance. Therefore, it thrives in America. I speak with so many people about this issue that I am always surprised at my own surprise. I am still surprised at each person who says to me, as if he or she were the person who thought of it first, "Why did she stay after he hit her?" But this ignorance should give us all hope—because once people know about domestic violence, just as they know they must vaccinate their children against polio, they will work to end it. We know that education will save the lives of children as well as their mothers. We must take small measures and know what domestic violence is about so we can lower the number of deaths that result from this terrible problem, and eventually end it completely. When you realize what it does to children, you'll be glad you read this far.

We make all kinds of noise in America about violence in movies and on television. But what has a greater impact on kids—violence, aggression, and verbal abuse on TV, or the same things right in the living room, live and between parents? Obviously, domestic violence creates violence in the streets. It makes women homeless with their children. It makes adults and children suffer.

Often the social welfare system deals with violence between partners by either ignoring it or blaming the mother. As you know by now, learned helplessness and brainwashing mean women often leave only to find themselves unable to support the children. So they go back, believing the man's false promise that he will change.

As I meet with lawyers and judges, as well as custody evaluators and shelter workers, I realize more and more that some of the people most ignorant about family violence are to be found in the legal system. Those making decisions about children and women trapped in the cycle of family violence must be educated. People must demand that judges, lawyers, doctors, and evaluators, along with police officers, learn how to help. The relative poverty of most victims of violence and the ignorance about domestic violence and its effect on children make this chapter a very important one. I write this from the heart: you cannot understand the problem by reading only this chapter. Read this whole book and then you will have all the pieces of the puzzle.

A child custody battle can be a part of an ongoing pattern of family violence. This pattern includes physical, financial, and emotional violence and control. The victim of domestic violence has likely been threatened with what might happen should she escape. The batterer may have threatened to kill her, the children, or family members.[2] He may threaten suicide, kidnapping, or a custody battle. In leaving him, she already faces an uphill financial battle, and without proper, well-trained legal counsel, she is likely to enter into a quick settlement, which may include giving the batterer regular child visitation. This will require her to be available to him so that he can get the children for visits.

Studies show that the most dangerous time for the victim comes when she has left her abuser.[3] Once a woman files for divorce and/or custody, she must have every support in order to see her safely through to the next stage of her journey to freedom. The legal system cannot help her if its members fail to understand the dynamics of batterer-victim relationships. Indeed, the pattern of violence at the *end* of such relationships has only recently been studied by social scientists.

One report found that the unrecognized area of violence occurs at the end of relationships.[4] The studies cited found that violence not only causes women to leave marriages and thus contributes to America's high divorce rate, but also continues to play a role during the divorce, as couples negotiate for assets.[5] One study was based on interviews of a random sample of 129 divorced women with children, drawn from 1986 divorce court records in Philadelphia.[6] For these women, leaving a violent relationship did not end the violence; in fact, 4 percent of the women who reported violence said it occurred only during the separation.[7] Eleven percent of the women who had experienced violence during marriage also experienced violence during the separation.[8] Four percent reported an immediate threat of violence: the husbands had forcibly entered their homes by breaking down the door and destroying property.[9]

Other researchers have reported high rates of abuse after separation. According to a 1993 survey, 19 percent of separated wives were physically abused by their husbands when they were separated.[10] Thirty-five percent of these women reported that their husbands became *more* violent after separation.[11] One study showed that more than a quarter of the women in divorce mediation reported postseparation threats of physical abuse or actual physical abuse.[12]

Custody blackmail is the term for a father's threat to sue for custody, even when he does not want it, to force the mother to bargain away her rights to spousal and child support.[13] The data compiled suggest that when women feared they could lose custody, during negotiations for child support they reduced their demands for resources.

One study stressed that its sample of fathers used threats to obtain custody as a way to control their wives. More than three-fourths of the seventy-five fathers threatened a custody challenge after the divorce, with nearly one-third issuing a formal threat through an attorney. The same study found that women who faced harassment during negotiations for custody also experienced it during visitation.[14]

The National Clearinghouse for the Defense of Battered Women reports that divorced and separated women are battered fourteen times as often as women still living with their partners and account for 75 percent of all battered women.[15] These women are not being battered by "other" men, but specifically by the men they are divorcing or leaving.[16]

Economic dependency, a common aspect of violent relationships, is also made worse by the financial needs of children, who may be supported by Aid to Families with Dependent Children (AFDC) and other government programs.[17] These programs barely cover basic expenses, and if a lawyer must be employed for a custody battle, it will outstrip the woman's resources and often those of her friends and family.

Unless the children are clearly at risk for a...
the courts should recognize custody disputes in...
cases for what they are: a litigation tactic rathe...
sion of concern for the best interests of the chi...
absence of clear legal guidelines, and given batte...
too-common lack of legal counsel, a battered wo... ...mily
court can be revictimized by the custody dispute. Failure to com-
prehend her point of view plays into the hands of the abusive parent, who most likely appears completely normal to all observers.[18]

As we have mentioned, the most commonly asked question
about the battered woman is "Why didn't she leave?" The question
suggests that the victim has an extensive list of options. Single,
childless women with funds can rent an apartment, relocate, and
take other protective measures suggested by experts in stalking.[19]
Women with children must fear for the children's safety and are
harassed by the possibility that the batterer will seek joint or sole
custody of the children when she leaves him.[20] Protective actions
for stalking victims include moving to an undisclosed location,
having an unlisted phone number, and changing one's name and
even Social Security number. These methods are clearly ineffec-
tive when one parent is ordered by a court to make children available for visits with the other parent who is stalking her.

Children are used as weapons and pawns by both men and women,
of course. But when the batterer threatens to take custody away
from a woman should she leave, evaluators and attorneys must see
that the custody battle itself can become a new arena for domestic abuse. Since the children may also have been threatened by the
abuser, the domestic violence must be understood by the courts
when there are children involved. The effect of the violence on children is a major factor, which must be brought to the attention of

...ts and legislators if we are to see any change in the current situation.

The effect of violence on children is well-documented, and while violence in movies and on television gets the high-profile attention of politicians and movie moguls, the impact of domestic violence on children has not been met with a similar response.[21] An estimated 87 percent of children in violent homes witness the abuse.[22] There is no doubt that the children are harmed in many ways—cognitive, psychological, and social—by observing or hearing brutality against a parent at home.[23]

Given the enormous impact witnessing violence has on children, it would seem common sense to expect the states to enact laws providing that, in the "best interest of the child," batterers be denied joint or sole custody until they successfully complete an appropriate therapy program.[24]

These facts must not keep the victim from seeking help. She should insist her lawyer read this book—especially this chapter, which has endnotes so that lawyers and social workers can easily identify the source of the information and add it to their reports and briefs. This is the only chapter in this book with endnotes, and they are here for a reason. We want to be certain that the information is used by lawmakers, lawyers, judges, and all the other people who are in a position to change laws. This means everyone!

To a family not suffering from domestic violence, a divorce is devastating enough, but for the victims of violence, divorce means ongoing contact with the abuser, expensive legal battles fraught with the fear of losing child custody, and expensive custody evaluations. An attorney's failure to recognize a victim's vulnerability in a divorce or separation puts her at risk.

The San Diego city attorney's domestic violence unit provides training sessions for police officers, judges, prosecutors, and volunteer attorneys.[25] A mandatory-arrest policy for batterers takes the burden off the victim, who otherwise often fears retaliation from the batterer if she demands or even agrees to his arrest.[26] Vigorous prosecutions can help a victim when she enters family court since she has proof—a criminal conviction—that he is a batterer. Proving abuse in family court is often very hard to do.

Some victims can find legal help through a lawyers' association or a clinic. But even well-paid lawyers can be almost useless when it comes to helping a battered woman. She must be strong and insist that her lawyer use the laws that are there to protect her. Aggressive lawyers who are familiar with those laws are often the answer to a battered woman's fear of leaving the abuser.

The law should smooth the road to safety and permit her sanctuary, while requiring the abusive partner to get counseling and, in extreme cases, providing for imprisonment if he continues to threaten or stalk her.

The nexus between spouse abuse and child abuse is well-documented.[27] The long-term impact of exposure to domestic violence is apparent from studies of male perpetrators of violence and female survivors of violence in adult relationships.[28] The majority of abusive husbands have grown up in families where they witnessed their fathers' abuse of their mothers.[29] Studies in this field suggest that the sons of severe batterers were ten times likelier to abuse their own wives as the sons of nonviolent fathers were.[30] Abused women are less likely to seek assistance if they have witnessed violence in their family of origin.[31] In many circumstances, children may be victimized along with the mother.[32] Conservative estimates indicate there is at least a 30 percent overlap between batterers who assault their women and those who abuse their children.[33]

Though many parents think their children are not aware of the violence, between 80 and 90 percent of children say otherwise.[34] At the horrifying extreme, in approximately 25 percent of cases where women are murdered by their husbands, children witness the crime.[35] Many children feel so responsible for their mother's safety that they adjust their own lives in order to protect her at all times, refusing to go to school.[36] Other children may feel it is their duty to defuse their father's anger.[37] They may feel this overwhelming responsibility from an early age; such a situation wreaks havoc on a child's social development, academic and community involvement, and sense of personal competence.[38]

In spite of such concerns, children often are a reason women stay in abusive relationships (other factors may include fear, economic dependency, self-blame, and lack of community support).[39] The abused mother may fear losing the children, as often the batterer has threatened either to kidnap them or to wage an expensive custody battle.[40] These fears are well-founded: some research suggests that abusive husbands have an excellent chance of convincing judges that they should have custody[41] and can destroy their partners economically to the point of rendering them homeless.[42]

Again, for a victim of violence: don't let this information keep you in the relationship. Use this book to help you get out, with the children. I have been there. I know how hard it is to read this. You are not to blame for his violence, but only you can free yourself and your children. If it's hard to read this, skip to Part Two and come back to this later.

Both common sense and expert opinion indicate spousal abuse is bad for children. One California court noted: "Every study reviewed by the committee indicates that spousal abuse is detrimental to children and must be considered a significant factor in custody decisions."[43]

In 1993 the American Bar Association Commission on Women in the Profession sent out a panel to various major cities to gather testimony from law students and professors. I asked to address the panel on the subject of legal education about domestic violence, a topic that baffled the commission but that they agreed to hear.

At a law firm in Manhattan, I spoke last, after several students and professors who discussed various topics. The panel members told me they did not understand my topic. I read them some statistics about domestic violence; they told me they believed such problems were being dealt with in the profession. I told them that during my family law course, which I took at the same time I took criminal law, the domestic violence cases we studied were all alike. In each, the woman was the accused murderer of the battering spouse. What does this tell us about how lawyers learn about domestic violence? Indeed, not a single case in either class had as its focus a woman who had been murdered by her spouse or former spouse.

I spoke about my own life experience in a violent marriage, in 1988. While trying to get my then-husband arrested for assault, I had spoken with several prosecutors, who told me that battered women, as far as they knew, were psychological cripples who often killed their husbands when they should simply have left the violent home.

The ABA commission frankly did not believe me when I told them that in Manhattan, a magnet for aspiring lawyers, only one law school out of five, Fordham, had an academic and clinical program in domestic violence. The audience of professors and students nodded their agreement. Somehow, the commission had believed, things were much better with "all the press" about domestic violence. After they realized how bad things are, the commission was deeply interested in what I had to say about domestic violence and law school education.

But the failure to have legal clinics devoted to family law and domestic violence is only a symptom of a larger problem in our law schools. Our textbooks and our attitudes need to address domestic violence as a root cause of violence elsewhere in our society. Interdisciplinary courses must be carefully combined with clinics to assure that students do not simply take a clinical course, glean some hands-on experience, and leave without learning the academic skills they must have in order to deal with the problem in their careers. Lawyers need research skills in disciplines such as medicine, psychology, sociology, and child development. As an example, California Western School of Law in San Diego offers an interdisciplinary two-semester course that deals with children and law. The course includes speakers, books, and internships, none of which deal exclusively with legal issues.[44]

One problem in starting such clinics is the unpopularity of victims of domestic violence. One trend I have found is that law school clinic courses may address the problem of child abuse while not assisting the domestic violence victim who is a parent. I attended a meeting of the American Bar Association's Center for Children in April 1994. The conference was well attended by children's rights advocates from all over America; not one of the presentations covered the need to represent a victim of violence in order to help her protect her children. The attitude is that an adult victim is responsible for protecting the child—but unless her difficulty in getting court-ordered custody or monitored visitation is addressed, the assumption that she can protect the child is simply false. (Again, to the victim: don't let this scare you. We are trying to change things by making people aware of how isolated you are, so that when you reach out for help, the help will be there.)

This chapter is about children. It is also, obviously, about the law. "We, the People," are the ones who make the law in America. We can tell our lawmakers that we want to protect not only the adult victims of domestic violence but also the children. We want America's dirty little secret out in the open so that we can take away the power it has over innocent lives.

The title of a *Los Angeles Times* article on domestic violence and pregnancy, by Shari Roan, really says it all: "A Dirty Secret: Society Would Like to Think That All Expectant Moms Are Cherished. But Pregnancy May Start—or Increase—Domestic Violence." Roan reports:

> *The beating of pregnant women may be the deepest secret in the dark world of domestic violence. It is hard to reconcile society's traditional response to a pregnant woman . . . with the image of a woman cowering in her own home, shielding her protruding abdomen from punches and kicks. . . .*
>
> *According to various studies, a disturbing number of pregnant women is [sic] physically abused. When 691 pregnant women in Houston and Baltimore were asked three simple questions about violence during a routine prenatal visit, 17% said they had been physically or sexually assaulted during the pregnancy; almost two-thirds of that percentage reported two or more beatings, according to the 1992 study in the* Journal of the American Medical Association.
>
> *And, in a 1994 study of 1,203 women screened on several occasions throughout pregnancy, 20.6% of teens and 14.2% of adults reported abuse. [A]dult women are most likely to be battered by male partners . . . noted the study, published in the journal* Obstetrics & Gynecology.

The article further reports:

The few studies that have been done on battering during pregnancy show two typical health consequences: Battered women are twice as likely to deliver a low-birth-weight baby (5.5 pounds or less) than women not abused and twice as likely to seek prenatal care only late in the pregnancy.

Other studies have shown that battering during pregnancy inhibits maternal weight gain, elevates the risk of infections, bleeding, and anemia, and may trigger smoking, drinking, and drug abuse in the mother.

And in one study of women who had experienced miscarriages, 7% reported being battered at some point during the pregnancy. Physical abuse may also lead some women to choose abortion, according to some psychiatric studies.

Many of the women I have spoken to about domestic violence report that the father of their child tried to talk them into abortion, often going back and forth in his feelings about the pregnancy right up to delivery. Imagine how terrible it is to carry a life within you while the father, to whom you look for support and affection now and in the future, threatens you and the child and perhaps beats you. Much of the abuse I heard about had less to do with wanting the woman to abort than it did with wanting to control a situation the batterer could not control. Some men veered between wanting the woman to abort and calling her a terrible mother, on the one hand, and on the other becoming angry if she actually did consider abortion. In my experience, this kind of man really feels a sense of power and control over life and death when his partner is pregnant. But his need to control the woman and his jealousy of the attention she may be getting lead him to have a shorter fuse than he has when she isn't pregnant. He may be more quickly prone to violence.

In "A Dirty Secret," reporter Shari Roan quotes Alana Bowman, a Los Angeles deputy city attorney who has prosecuted domestic violence since 1972. "There is so much we don't know about domestic violence," Bowman told Roan. She estimated that pregnant women are victims in about 20 percent to 30 percent of the misdemeanor cases she handles, and she believes that, to the batterer, pregnancy represents "a threatening change in the relationship.

"When you talk to . . . batterer[s], they say they feel the stress of the pregnancy," Bowman says. "But we also find that these are excuses or a rationale for men to have a primary position in the relationship. What the baby represents is the moving-aside of the man in his primacy. . . . The pregnancy is a threat to him because she has to go to the doctor every month; there are more people who can influence her. The baby is the focus of her life now, not him. She is getting attention from more people."

One victim asked the reporter, "If you knew that [if] you didn't do exactly what you were told, when you were told . . . [the fetus] would be the target of violence, how intimidated would you be?"

Doctors are surprisingly ignorant of the problem, reports Roan:

"When I [speak] about this to physicians' groups and health-care providers, they are always surprised to hear battering is common during pregnancy and that it sometimes begins during pregnancy," said Dr. Elaine J. Alpert, a Boston University medical school professor and author of a recent article on domestic violence in the Annals of Internal Medicine. *. . . Alpert says that all women should be asked about domestic abuse during prenatal care and again before they are discharged from the hospital after delivery. . . . [Some] women welcome the inquiries, says Dr. Michael Wilkes, cofounder of a domestic violence course for medical students at UCLA. . . .*

Experts say the batterer will often accompany the woman to the emergency room or doctor's office and will try to answer questions for her or curtail what she says.[45]

My experience supports this: at a clinic in Laguna Beach, California, doctors and nurses told me that batterers often insist on staying with the patient during exams in pregnancy.

During my last pregnancy, which resulted in the birth of my youngest son, I was often urged to have an abortion when I told my doctors and nurses about the domestic violence. But this wasn't the advice I wanted! If a woman has indeed chosen to continue the pregnancy and is getting prenatal care, it is the height of unkindness to suggest she terminate the pregnancy. Why not instead encourage her to make contact with local shelters and legal services? Choice in reproduction has to mean that when one decides to carry a child to term, one will not be badgered or second-guessed about the wisdom of the decision. Most health professionals would not do such a thing if the choice is abortion.

I do not want to imply that I oppose legal and safe abortion. But when we make the choice to carry the child to term, we ask for respect from our health-care providers. *A battered pregnant woman needs referrals to services for battered women;* the advice to abort is not a substitute.

Even after I gave birth to my youngest child, health-care providers said things like, "Well, if he [my ex-husband] was really that bad, why did you have this baby instead of an abortion?" Think about it: you're holding a baby and being asked why you gave birth to him instead of choosing abortion. It's a pretty sad example of how we've forgotten simple courtesy and the art of polite conversation. (By the way, he's an adorable child and I'm sure he'll contribute wonderful things in this world. The same is true of my other two.)

A second *Los Angeles Times* article, Geraldine Baum's "The Forgotten Victims," details the effects family violence has on children:

Every year at least 3 million American children 3 to 17 are exposed to this at-home violence, according to Richard Gellis, a University of Rhode Island professor who has spent 25 years researching domestic violence. . . .

Older children and teenagers tend to try to get in between their parents in what has been dubbed "the Bill Clinton phenomenon." As a young teen, Clinton reportedly stood up to his mother's second husband several times, but on one pivotal occasion in 1960 grabbed his stepfather by the arm, looked him in the eye, and said, "Hear me. Never ever touch my mother again." . . .

The children who seem to suffer the most are ages 5 to 10, according to most experts. They know what's going on but they're too little and too weak to do anything about it. They experience hopelessness and sometimes thoughts of suicide; they often get headaches and stomachaches; they can become utterly passive and numb, or uncontrollably violent.

To recover, a child needs careful counseling, or at least a special relationship with an empathetic person.

Baum concludes:

Whatever the age of the child, the solutions are the same: therapy, a mother who gets help for herself, a caretaker who is nurturing, sympathetic day care and schools that offer a stable environment.

The challenge for school officials and day-care workers is often excavating the truth about what's going on at home. One barrier is that it's just so embarrassing and confusing to children that their parents' anger can escalate out of control.[46]

It is hard to write these words. It must be hard to read them. But all of us together can save lives. If the U.S. Department of Justice and the Federal Bureau of Investigation are right (and they are probably very conservative), three or four women a day are killed by husbands or boyfriends, or former husbands and boyfriends. San Diego, as we've mentioned, has reduced its domestic violence death rate by 60 percent. Imagine. The city accomplished that through education.

Encourage others to get familiar with the facts about violence and the solutions that we know work. Teach one another. Insist that your police station, your county family court, and your law schools, medical schools, preschools, and Sunday schools use this book or one like it to shed light on what has been, up until now, a dirty secret. Together we can save lives.

Education will work, because it can improve every kind of service. Those who are already working to solve the problem will be thrilled that people are "getting it." We see the effect domestic violence has on innocent life, on our precious children. We cannot ignore it.

Notes

1. Metro Desk, "Deputies Describe Chaos After Woman's Slaying at Courthouse," *Los Angeles Times* (March 13, 1996).

2. B. Carter Thompson, "Defending the Battered Wife," *Trial* (Feb. 1984), pp. 74, 76 (discussing the myriad of reasons compelling the woman to stay with the batterer, including social, psychological, religious, legal, and financial pressures).

3. Joan Pennington, "Family Law Developments," *Clearinghouse Review,* vol. 25 (1992), p. 1159.

4. Demie Kurz, "Separation, Divorce, and Woman Abuse," *Violence Against Women* (March 1996), pp. 63, 65–67.

5. Ibid., pp. 63–65.

6. Ibid., pp. 65–68.

7. Ibid., p. 69.

8. Ibid.

9. Ibid.

10. Kurz, op. cit., p. 69, citing Johnson, H., and Sacco, V., "Researching Violence Against Women: Statistics Canada National Survey," *Canadian Journal of Criminology*, vol. 37, no. 3 (1995), pp. 281–304.

11. Ibid.

12. Ibid., citing Ellis, D., and N. Stuckless, "Post-Separation, Marital Conflict Mediation, and Post-Separation Abuse," *Mediation Quarterly*, vol. 9 (1992), pp. 205–209.

13. Kurz, op. cit., p. 76.

14. Ibid., citing Arendell, T., *Fathers and Divorce: At the Intersection of Family and Gender* (Sage Publications, 1995).

15. From the Legislative History of S.B. 924, 1995, passed into law as California Code of Civil Procedure § 340.15.

16. Telephone interview with a sponsor of S.B. 924, Julliette Markowitz (June 11, 1996).

17. Del Martin, *Battered Wives* (Pocket Books, a division of Simon & Schuster, 3d ed., 1983), p. 120.

18. Those not trained to recognize the dynamics of domestic violence may be easily lulled by men who batter their wives; to those outside the family, such men often don't come across as abusive individuals. Often, the abusive man maintains a public image as a friendly, caring person and a devoted "family man." David Adams, "Identifying the Assaultive Husband in Court: You Be the Judge," *Boston Bar Journal*, vol. 33 (1989), p. 23. Many batterers effectively use this suave exterior to maintain continued control over their victims and children by successfully manipulating the court process. As a result, batterers' rates of success in obtaining custody of their children at a contested custody trial may be somewhat higher than nonbatterers', who succeed 38 to 63 percent of the time. See Nancy D. Polikoff, "Child Custody Decisions: Exploring the Myth That Mothers Always Win," *Women's Rights Law Reporter*, vol. 7 (1982), pp. 235, 236–37.

19. Notes from the Stalking Conference, given in San Diego by the district attorney's office, at the University of San Diego (April 1996).

20. Carla Fischer, Neil Vidmar, and Rene Ellis, "The Culture of Battering and the Role of Mediation in Domestic Violence Cases," *Southern Methodist University Law Review* (summer 1993), pp. 2117, 2155.

21. Howard Davidson, ed., *Domestic Violence and Children: A Report to the President of the American Bar Association* (August 1994), p. 1.

22. Ibid., citing Harrell, Adele, National Council of Juvenile and Family Court Judges, *A Guide to Research on Family Violence* (1993), p. 28.

23. Ibid.

24. "Although it may seem that the mother's decision to leave will protect her children from further exposure to violence and its effects, the continuing involvement of the batterer in the lives of both the children and their mother may create new problems, exacerbate old problems, and prevent healing of the damage that has already occurred. Given that the man's need for power and control is an important component of domestic violence, divorce may actually exacerbate his need to control, as evidenced in bitter and never ending custody disputes." Marsha B. Liss and Geraldine Butts Stahly, eds., *Battering and Family Therapy* (Sage Publications, 1993), p. 175.

25. Casey G. Gwinn and Sgt. Anne O'Dell, "Stopping the Violence: The Role of the Police Officer and the Prosecutor," 20 *Western State University Law Review* (1993), p. 1501.

26. Ibid., p. 1513.

27. Nancy K. D. Lemon, *Domestic Violence and Children: Resolving Custody and Visitation Disputes, A National Judicial Curriculum* (The Family Violence Prevention Fund, 1995), p. 22, citing Gelles, R. J., and M. A. Straus, *Intimate Violence* (Simon & Schuster, 1988), and Walker, L. E., "Psychology and Violence Against Women," *American Psychologist*, vol. 44, no. 4 (1989), pp. 695–702.

28. Ibid.

29. Ibid.

30. Ibid.

31. Ibid.

32. Ibid.

33. Ibid., p. 22, citing Jaffe, P. G., D. Wolfe, and S. Wilson, *Children of Battered Women* (Sage Publications, 1990); and Schechter, S., and J. L. Edelsen, "In the Best Interest of Women and Children: A Call for Collaboration Between Child Welfare and Domestic Violence Constituencies," paper presented at the Domestic Violence and Child Welfare Conference, Racine, Wisconsin (June 1994).

34. Ibid, p. 21, citing Jaffe, P. G., et al. (see above, note 33).

35. Ibid, p. 22, citing Crawford, M., and R. Gartner, *Women Killing, Intimate Femicide in Ontario: 1974–1990* (Toronto: The Women We Honor Action Committee, 1992).

36. Ibid, p. 22, citing Peled, E., "The Experience of Living with Violence for Preadolescent Child Witnesses of Woman Abuse," unpublished doctoral dissertation, University of Minnesota, Minneapolis (1993); and Jaffe, P. G., et al., op. cit. (see above, note 33).

37. Ibid.

38. Ibid.

39. Ibid., p. 23.

40. Ibid.

41. Joan Zorza, "Mandatory Arrest for Domestic Violence: Why It May Prove the Best First Step in Curbing Repeat Abuse," *ABA Criminal Justice,* vol. 3, no. 10 (fall 1995), pp. 2, 53.

    Where both parents were arrested, the father, having more access to jobs, money, and friends, was almost always able to leave jail immediately, whereas the mother, typically unable to post bail, remained incarcerated until trial. Many of these mothers lost custody of their children. At the very least, these mothers lost any advantage that statutes making domestic violence a factor in custody disputes were meant to give them, despite the fact that four-fifths of the states have enacted such statutes to offer just such protection. Children who had called the police experienced considerable guilt for having precipitated any arrest, especially when their mother was arrested. When their mother was inappropriately arrested, the children were further harmed because they learned that their abusive fathers could successfully manipulate the system, and that nobody came to their victimized mother's aid. Furthermore, some of them were terrified by being placed in foster care or in the abuser's care.

42. Moreover, studies consistently indicate that approximately 50 percent of homeless women with children are fleeing domestic violence. Joan Zorza, "Woman Battering: A Major Cause of Homelessness," *Clearinghouse Review* (special issue, 1991), p. 421. In other words, many women have nowhere to go with their children.

Finally, help for battered women who seek safety is rarely forthcoming, from either official or unofficial sources. See Edward Gondolf and Ellen Fisher, *Battered Women as Survivors: An Alternative to Treating Learned Helplessness* (1988). More than 7 percent of women studied had left home at some time in response to violence; substantial numbers sought help of various kinds, help that was not forthcoming. Mary Ann Dutton, "Understanding Women's Response to Domestic Violence: A Redefinition of Battered Woman Syndrome," 21 *Hofstra Law Review* (1993), pp. 1191,1227, surveying social science literature, confirms that "battered women utilize an impressive array of strategies for attempting to stop the violence in some way."

43.   In re Benjamin D, 227 Cal. App. 3d 1464, 1468, 278 *Cal. Rptr.* 468, 470 (1991). All California family courts are required by California Family Code §3011 to take domestic violence into consideration in deciding the best interests of the children in custody cases. Unfortunately, evaluators often do not recognize domestic violence, and when they do, judges have a hard time dealing with it. Education of lawyers, judges, and custody evaluators is a purpose of this book. If you're reading this endnote, and you're a member of the legal profession, you have a special responsibility to use the information in this book to help save lives.

44.   Interview with Professor Janet Weinstein, California Western School of Law, who teaches the course (March 1996).

45.   Shari Roan, "A Dirty Secret: Society Would Like to Think That All Expectant Moms Are Cherished. But

Pregnancy May Start—or Increase—Domestic Violence," *Los Angeles Times* (December 5, 1995).

46. Geraldine Baum, "The Forgotten Victims: Every Year at Least 3 Million American Children Witness the Battering or Killing of One of Their Parents. They Rarely Get Over the Trauma," *Los Angeles Times* (July 20, 1994).

Part 2

Letters to the Battered Woman

A Domestic Violence "Thermometer"

The gauge that follows is not a substitute for professional advice. You may need a social worker, a therapist, a lawyer, or other assistance. If you are in danger, call 911 or a battered women's shelter. But if you are not sure if your relationship is "that bad," read over the different levels of control and abuse, and see how much of what we say is familiar to you.

Violent people can change, but *your first goal is to protect yourself and your family*. If the "temperature" of your relationship is high, you may want to make plans to leave home or the relationship. If things are still pretty "cool," but there are danger signs, it is possible to seek therapy and learn to strengthen your self-esteem. If these efforts make the danger "temperature" go up—if the response is threats or acts of violence—take the next step and leave. Please don't feel pushed by this advice; it is only advice, and it's not meant to force you into quick decisions. This violence thermometer may give you just enough distance from your own pain and numbness to help you begin to heal. We encourage you to read the whole book if you are safe enough to do it, or to get to a shelter and read it there!

Low-Temperature Behavior: Danger Signs

— — — — — — — — — — — — — — —

62°

He is jealous of other men or women. You feel responsible for this and try to avoid looking at other people so as not to set off an argument.

65°

He wants you to quit your job or to move in with him even though you don't feel really comfortable with that. You may feel secretly pleased by his interest in your situation. You may feel he really cares and wants to protect you by having you leave a job you don't love, or wants to save money on rent by moving in. But those little feelings of uncertainty should not be ignored!

68°

He is always telling you how you feel, and while it seems supportive and caring, you always feel you've been criticized, kind of indirectly.

70°

He actually checks to see how long you have been grocery shopping or on the phone with another person. He may even check the odometer in your car and make crazy-seeming comments about where you have been and what you are doing. Seems kind of paranoid—but you figure he just really loves you. Right? Hmmm . . . maybe there's more to this problem?

72°

He isolates you from your family and friends. You may feel really happy that he cares; maybe you have problems with those people, and you feel he is helping you by being there for you. But isolation is not good: it makes you dependent

75°

on him. These behaviors between 62° and 78° are all "beginning" signs.

He criticizes your makeup or clothing. He may buy you clothes you don't especially like (or clothes you really do like). You may wonder why he doesn't want you to wear certain kinds of clothes. He may try to get you to look kind of dumpy—then, later, criticize you for looking just that way. This kind of control over your appearance is not healthy for your self-esteem!

78°

He may try to get you to quit school—or he may try to push you into a course of study you don't really like. He may encourage you to go to school, then complain that you are too busy for him. You can expect to feel kind of confused.

80°

He has a mean temper. Other people tell you not to get him angry. Maybe he has told you he used to be mean, but he has changed. If he has not completed an extensive therapy with a good anger-management therapist, know that you are in a new level of danger. This guy is in *deep denial,* and you don't want to be there with him.

85°

He has a record of arrest for spouse abuse, or assault, or any kind of crime involving violence or threats. This guy must get therapy if you are ever to be sure he can be trusted.

88°

He is really quiet. Really, really quiet. He doesn't make threats, he doesn't lose his temper. He just withholds love, affection, and encouragement, and you feel empty, though everything else is okay in your relationship. This is one of the most painful kinds of abuse because it is probably not intentional and leaves no bruises. He really needs to open up and learn to express his love. This is in the danger zone because your relationship will change as you begin to learn to expect love and affection from your partner. He may get really threatened if it happens. Watch out for the "silent knight" kind of man.

90°

He openly threatens you if you do things he doesn't want you to do. If he tells you to quit your job and you don't, he says he will lose his temper and "won't be responsible for his actions." He tells you if you wear that outfit one more time and he finds out about it, you're "in trouble." He may not be specific, but the fact that he threatens you at all is a strong warning sign.

Higher Temperature

95°

He tells you what he will do if you don't follow his "rules": he will hit you, destroy your property, hurt someone you love, call your friends or family members and tell them awful things about you. He tells you he will kill you. He may not seem very angry when he says this, and you may feel more numb than frightened. *Be frightened!* Do something. (Don't confront him; just keep reading and look for a way out.)

98°

He has hurt you, or he criticizes you so much it's like verbal torture. He calls you bad things; he tells you you're everything from a whore to the devil incarnate. He blames you for his problems and punishes you for them. This stage is a little hotter than the one just before.

100°

You walk on eggshells. His rules seem to change all the time. He has humiliated you in front of friends and family. Other people have even commented on this, and that makes you feel worse. On the other hand, he may treat you like gold in front of other people, but like dirt when you're alone.

Really Hot Situation

105°

He is very strong or has access to guns or has had special martial-arts training. He has threatened to kill or hurt you, but has not actually hit you. He has spent time in the army or the police, or has a history of criminal activity. You may be an army wife or a policeman's wife or even a fireman's wife. He may be a pillar of your community, and you feel you won't be believed.

108°

He has hit you very hard or pushed you into walls. You know he is an abusive man. You go through periods where everything is just fine, but you are always afraid he'll lose his temper.

110°

You have called 911 or tried to get into a shelter. You have talked with counselors, pastors, friends, or doctors. You may have been treated for bruises, cuts, and scrapes as a result of the abuse. He may even have broken a bone or your eardrum.

112°

You have missed work as a result of abuse. You have canceled plans because of fights. You are afraid. You're thinking of getting out. *Good for you!*

115°

You have been hospitalized. He may have been arrested. *Do not take him back* before (1) he does a treatment program, and (2) he is given a clean bill of health. Get your own counseling and be independent. Let him back into your life only on a limited basis: these guys are really hard to treat. Remember, recovery is 50 percent, at best.

118°

You've separated from him. He threatens to kill you and has beaten you. He threatens to kidnap your children, hurt your parents, or break into your house. Maybe he has broken into the house. Make sure you have good restraining orders and that your police force knows about them. Consider being in a shelter and getting permission to keep your address a secret. Do whatever it takes to stay safe.

120°

He stalks you. He goes to your workplace, your school, your church. He is like your shadow. He makes you feel extremely uncomfortable, whatever the history of violence has been. Get a restraining order, have him served with it, and tell your employer, your school's security, your neighbors—*everyone*—about it. If, in spite of the restraining order, he shows up in a café when you are having coffee, and so much as looks at you, call the police and get him arrested. Nip the little violations in the bud, and make a record of the abuse as soon as it is safe for you to do so.

Strengthening from the Inside

> *The most powerful weapon in the hands of an*
> *oppressor is the mind of the oppressed.*
> —STEVE BIKO, SOUTH AFRICAN POLITICAL LEADER

We were queens. Queens of De Nile.
—A MEMBER OF MY SUPPORT GROUP

When I first began to realize I was being abused, *everything I read about battering relationships seemed to blame the victim.* If you are in an abusive relationship, or are coming out of one, you may even feel there is a bit of that in this book. We are trying to give you information and practical help, so please forgive us if some of it sounds like blame.

Especially when we discuss the spiritual side of this problem and the need to take back your power, it may seem as if we're saying, "Hey! There's something wrong with part of you that needs fixing." But that's not what we say in this chapter at all.

The fact is, an abuser has hurt you inside; maybe there have been physical assaults too. So before you leave the relationship, be sure you are strong enough and healed enough to make that final step stick.

If you are in danger right now, you'll probably want to just take this book and get yourself into a shelter. If things are bad, but you haven't made that final decision, take the time to build up your inner self and make some practical moves to protect yourself after you go.

This letter is about your inner needs and how to meet them. The other letters cover things like getting into a shelter and getting your life back together. We are starting with the spiritual not because we think you aren't spiritual—far from it! It's because spiritual work is *how you free your mind from oppression,* and in doing that, you'll take away much of the power he has to control you.

As a practical matter, begin to take in his verbal abuse through a filter. Don't start saying things like "Oh, now you're verbally abusing me. This must stop." This is the kind of nonsense advice therapists often gave me back in the late 1980s. Don't bother with that, just begin by hearing what he is really saying. Here are some decoded messages:

He says: "You're a filthy slob and a bad mother."
Translation: "I am desperate to control you and this is how I can do it. I will insult you."

He says: "You're ugly and fat."
Translation: "I am deeply insecure and think I am ugly. And I know if I say this you'll feel really, really bad."

He says: "You spend too much money."
Translation: "I am so afraid of losing control I just really need to push your buttons."

You get the idea.

As you hear him say these vicious things—and we know he says worse things than the examples we've given—just remember, you can *try to de-escalate.* You can try, for now at least, to keep him from going off the deep end and start hitting you.

Now doesn't that sound like I'm saying you're in control? But you're not. You're being victimized by a crazy person. I am just saying that *if* you can, try to keep him from losing it. If you succeed, you'll only have a temporary tool. Don't think you have become a controller, because you won't be able to keep this up for long and stay healthy. For now, use these methods to buy some time.

If he starts getting angry—and you know the signs better than I do—try to get to a room where there is an exit to the outside. If he has guns, keep him out of that room if you can. If the kitchen has two entries, try going in there. Say things like "You know, I really want to listen to you," or my old favorite (this one got me through some hairy moments), "Can I get us both a cup of tea? I do want to hear what you have to say. It's really important."

The point is, you let him know you are going to hear him out. You give him a cup of tea or coffee or a snack, and sit quietly. Nod, agree, sigh, let him know you are hearing him. Let him rant. Do not argue. Agree, if you can. If you just can't (he says you're unfaithful; you can't really agree with that one)—well, just say something like "I'm sorry you think that, it makes me feel so sad." *Don't let him get you upset!*

Try to detach; look at the two of you as if you were watching two people from a distance. What would you tell the woman to do? Maybe you'd say, "Leave!" Or maybe you'd say, "Stay calm, make plans to leave, leave when it is safe and you are ready to go."

If he hits you, curl up into a ball if you can. Try to get into a safe place like a neighbor's house or another part of your own house. Remember, you have done nothing wrong, he's the one committing the crime. You are now in the process of getting free and safe.

Pick some affirmations for yourself. Yes, those dumb positive-thinking things.

My own personal favorite (I reveal this only to you, the people who will read this and hopefully not make fun of me!) is (how embarrassing . . .): "Good girl!" Yes, folks, it got me through some really bad times. If I made the beds, I'd say, "Good girl!" If I was feeling terrible about my children, but I had gotten through a day's work or a day of school, I'd pull myself out of the dumps or pat myself on the back with that "Good girl" thing. Okay, I felt pretty dumb, but it worked for me.

What makes you feel good about yourself? Did you win an award in grade school or did someone tell you that you had pretty ears? Well, maybe you could repeat something like that to yourself. Or tell yourself, "I am a very nice person and I deserve a happy life." It is true, isn't it?

Prayer is very important. I know this will make some of you uncomfortable. A loving God wouldn't let a person suffer, would He? Well, admit to God you're angry and wait quietly for the response. I once read this little book entitled *May I Hate God?* by Pierre Wolf. It really spoke to me about hating God for the insane things that happen to us and are out of our control. Most of all, what it did was help me understand God in my suffering.

I got through some pretty bad times by prayer and meditation, and even through the roughest times of my life, after my ex-husband took our sons to Iran. Prayer and meditation are like talking and listening. They open your mind and spirit to the infinite wisdom and grace of God.

Personally, I am a Christian. Turning my life and will over to God is a daily task. I fail every single day in the task of being like Christ, being forgiving, loving, trusting, and faithful to my God. Every Christian I know is in the same boat. But whoever your God is, be sure you begin to pray and listen. Remember that your abuser is trying to destroy God's beloved child—you.

Of course, my former husband always told me he was trying to help me by criticizing and hitting me. It took me some time to understand that this was just his way of hurting me while still letting himself think he was a good husband. He thought he was beating me for my own good. The person hurting you may be anywhere from a mild-mannered nut to a real monster. But you must learn to keep faithful and honest with yourself. These little hints may sound silly, but if you try them, at least one of them will work for you.

You don't have to join an Eastern religion to meditate. God is everywhere. Everything around us has some form or design. It came from somewhere. It's going somewhere else. The fingerprints of God are all around us. You can pray, let go, breathe quietly in a safe place (he's gone, the house is quiet, you're at work or out shopping), and relax. Open yourself to peace. Ask God to speak, to heal, to become one with you. Ask God into your life. Sounds a little weird if you've never done it. But finding that still place in yourself can give you a place to run to if you feel terribly frightened or overwhelmed. You can stop, whatever happens, and go to that place.

You may want to imagine a very beautiful and special place, maybe a real place you liked. My personal favorite (I can hear you moan, "Not again!") is my grade school library, at El Morro Elementary in Laguna Beach. Okay, that's not your cup of tea. It no longer exists anyway, except in my mind and memory, circa 1967. Another place I like is Tobago, a lovely island where I took a much-needed winter break from New York. I remember looking out at Goat Island, where Ian Fleming wrote James Bond novels. If you can't think of a real place, make one up. Either way, go to that place in your mind, breathe some lovely scents—perfume or a flower—and think of nothing but peace. Quiet the noise of your mind. Let go of the moment; open yourself to wisdom and peace. Open your spirit to courage and grace, to honesty and happiness. Open your soul to beauty, to love, to God and who He wants you to become. You may feel slightly ridiculous when you first try it, but it's so good for you. It really sets you up for some positive thinking and gets you ready to make changes in your life. Let go of fear, and let go of negative thoughts about yourself. Nice, isn't it?

If you can, find help in your church or temple. You probably won't be able to find a good support group there, but you may be fortunate. Maybe you'll try to talk to your priest, rabbi, or pastor, but get nowhere. If so, remember that these are only people. God has plans for you that you cannot begin to understand. So if a spiritual adviser, a friend, or a member of your family can't understand what you're going through, don't let it get you down.

You may want to share this book with people—maybe give a copy to your pastor or lawyer. If you agree with one part but not with another, tell them so. (You have my complete permission to do this, of course!) Asking other people to read this book can help you create an informed support system. This is critical to creating your inner and outer escape. And it is an important route to recovery.

Laughter and hobbies, exercise and classes—these things may be beyond you at this point, but you will eventually find time for all those little things that used to make you happy.

In fact, humor can help you or hurt you. It can lift your spirits, especially when you've left the relationship and you hit a hard patch in the road to safety. But humor can also make you put a silver lining in every dark cloud.

This is what *denial* is about. "De Nile" is what we battered women are queens of. We tend to wait for things to get better when they just won't. The longer you wait to get out of a really bad relationship, the harder it can be.

You may have thought for years that he will change, but he hasn't. Or he does change, but then relapses. Or you're afraid and walking on eggshells, even though he hasn't hit you in years.

You're not a zombie, so don't spend your life as one of the living dead! You must wake up—and *if you have read this far, you are already getting out of the denial* that has kept so many of us only half alive.

About support groups: some are better than others. It may be impossible for you to get to one at this point, but do find out about them. You may need Alcoholics Anonymous if you drink too much; or, if your partner is an alcoholic, you need Al-Anon. If you have teenagers, there are teen Al-Anon programs to help understand the madness of living in a family where alcohol is abused. And there are wonderful support groups for adult children of alcoholics. Through these groups you can often meet people who can help you in your program of getting safe.

But if you can't get to a meeting or a program, you can still pray and meditate. *You can take away the abuser's single most powerful weapon.* And you don't have to tell him you're doing it. Remember, his most powerful weapon is your mind and how he uses it to hurt you. Don't let him push your buttons. You will have to provide your own detailed version of this grand basic model plan for recovery from abusive relationships—maybe your plan includes a counselor, a lawyer, a shelter, and an education. Maybe you need to save a little money somehow to make your getaway. But *having decided you are worthy of a far happier life is a first step*. It's important even if you have already left the relationship and are looking for a way to heal.

I believe firmly that you can take this first step to recovery. You can learn to trust yourself, to have faith in yourself and bit by bit in other people, and in a God who is perfect—even if we have been good faithful godly people and our lives are a complete disaster. We can learn to trust that in spite of all appearances, God loves us. And that He or (okay, you pagans) She does not want us to be abused.

This may sound extremely basic, even dumb. Maybe it's a repeat of advice other people have given you. But do this prayer/meditation/affirmation program for a while, and use the next few chapters to plan your path to freedom and healing. Remember, many of us have been there and are now working on hotlines, in shelters, and in many professions. And if you keep meeting people who blame you for the abuse or for the problems in the relationship, just turn them over like pancakes, to God or to your Higher Power, for fine-tuning. You are getting free. You may want to share this book with them, but if they are really unsupportive, find other people who will be kind to you. *Reach out* carefully, and *reach inward,* where the strength, wisdom, and beauty are.

Okay, you have a prayer/meditation program, or you're reading the Psalms; maybe you have a support group at church or elsewhere. You have your affirmation. You know some temporary survival tips and tools. Now you're ready to start planning.

Dealing with the Legal System

"How will I find help? How do I deal with the police? Where am I going to get a lawyer? Will the district attorney understand my case? Will the judge?"

So many times we are afraid to make that first step to recovery because we are afraid of the legal system. It has some pretty spectacular failures—cases where the batterer is let off with a slap on his wrist and later murders his victim. But the system more often, quietly, works. And things are getting better. This chapter is not about horror stories, but instead will give you some basic understanding of *how the system works.*

I learned much of this during my days as a victim, and it actually helped me both when I started working for lawyers and later, in law school. I find that people going through court, whether it's criminal court or family court or even civil court, feel better if they can understand some of the mysterious parts of it.

Right now, you may be wondering: "What is she talking about—civil, criminal, and family court?" If you're like me when I was first looking for help, you probably think court is court. In this letter I'll explain the difference, do my best to help you make the system work for you, and give you some tips on finding a good lawyer.

This section is not a substitute for a lawyer, but it may make the "legal" part of your journey to freedom and safety easier and less expensive. You may want to ask your lawyer to read this book in order to be sure he or she knows something about domestic violence.

If your husband or the father of your children has any money at all, you need a lawyer to protect your property rights and your right to custody of your children. He probably has access to your bank accounts and may have gotten you financially dependent on him. If you do call 911 and get him arrested, get your hands on the money and financial records before he gets out of jail. Of course, if it is a life-or-death situation, run! But one friend had her husband arrested over the weekend and didn't have a chance to call a lawyer. Her husband got out of jail and drained their bank accounts. She asked me to tell this story so someone could benefit from her hardship.

One advocacy group tells you to photocopy birth certificates and other documents so you can make a fast getaway with copies. Well, let me tell you something: many states require someone applying for benefits or a Social Security card to have certified originals of such documents. So *take everything you can get your hands on,* or get whatever certified copies you need and take those. If you go to a shelter, take with you all the cash, credit cards, and jewelry, or whatever you can. I know I'll be criticized for saying that, but I have seen it happen that a woman has to go home to get her driver's license and finds the batterer waiting for her. He might get violent, or he might sweet-talk her into coming back. One member of my support system photocopied her abuser's paychecks and their bank statements. Another got her husband to give her a lovely gold necklace and sold it to pay for an attorney. You know, those first months on your own will depend on money. So be practical, and if at all possible, save some money secretly. Sounds pretty crass—but if you have kids, you know how much it costs to care for them.

However, don't let money or the lack of it stop you. *Much of the legal help you need can be gotten free of charge, if you know where to find it.*

The next bits of advice are no substitute for law school. But they may help you when you are dealing with your lawyer or the legal system, whether it is the police, the criminal system, or the family court. Please look at the Suggested Reading list on page 194 for more books to help you understand what's happening as you go through the system. I can't emphasize enough the old saying "Knowledge is power."

However, don't go borrowing these books from libraries, or buying them, and leaving them around for your husband to see. You will be thinking, "He'll see I'm planning a divorce, and he'll change." How do I know that's what you're thinking? Been there, tried that, done that, didn't work, now I have wisdom to see into your mind and know you might try it. Don't work on changing him. Instead, *be strong, free your mind and soul, free your body from his abuse, and get on with your life.*

The difference between the criminal and civil court systems is this: in the criminal system, the government will put the criminals in jail or fine them. The civil system doesn't put anyone in jail unless a person in court refuses to follow an order given by the court. So in the criminal system, you have the state or federal government arresting people and putting them on trial. The defendant in a criminal trial has some really special rights, which are provided for in our Constitution: a fair and speedy trial, an attorney if the defendant is poor (not-so-poor people have to pay for their own lawyers, obviously), and the right not to be forced to testify against himself or herself. The government has to prove its case all by itself, beyond a reasonable doubt. This means the government can't expect the defendant to provide evidence, and it must do the job of convincing either a judge or a jury that the defendant is guilty.

Domestic violence was once considered only a family problem—one that families should solve. Finally the laws began to change and police and prosecutors slowly began to realize what women's groups have been saying for years: domestic violence is a crime, and if the victims are not protected, they may go back to the abuser and the abuse may end in homicide. To get this system to work for you, *get the abuser arrested or get a restraining order* (this is also called a TRO, an order of protection, or a protective order). Usually shelters can tell you how and where to get one.

Some courts have "victim witness" programs that will help you get orders. In California, the victim witness program pays medical expenses, counseling, and other expenses for crime victims. Your state may have a similar program. Sometimes, especially in big cities, you can go to court in the middle of the night and get a judge to sign your order. Sometimes the police will help you get one. You will often need to write an *affidavit* to attach to the order. The affidavit is a clear explanation of what happened.

If violence has happened before in your relationship, say so in the affidavit! If he has threatened you in the past, say so in the affidavit! If he has threatened family members or your children or someone else, say so in the affidavit! One lawyer told me that *the affidavit is the place to put in evidence that you may not be able to offer at any other time.* He recalled a woman whose abuser tore out a hunk of her hair. She put it into a Ziploc bag, and they stapled it to the affidavit.

If he has firearms, guns, knives, any kind of weapon, say so in the affidavit. If he is a drug abuser or alcoholic, say so. The judge will want to know why you want the restraining order, so be sure you make it clear. I realize that you must be thinking, "What, is she nuts, telling me to be an expert? I'm scared out of my wits!" I'm giving you the best information I have been able to get out of victims, shelters, and lawyers who work on domestic violence cases. I trust you will do the right thing, and ask a hundred questions of everyone in your support system, or look for answers when you can.

"Service of process" is a part of what we are guaranteed in our U.S. Constitution—it means we must be given notice of an action taken by a court and we must have an opportunity to be heard by that court. So, you have him served and you keep a proof of service to show the court. Sometimes you can get the order served on him by a sheriff. Some shelters do it themselves. A good attorney, shelter, or police officer can help you with these orders and getting them served.

You may need to appear in court and tell a judge why you need this order. Or an attorney will do it for you. You may feel terrified, but remember, many judges have been trained to deal with domestic violence, and all of them have seen victims of violence before. *Don't be afraid of the judge.* Tell your story calmly, but don't be afraid to show emotion if you're really shaken. Don't try to be strong; it may come across as coldness. *Show your fear and try to be somewhere between calm and hysterical.* Stay cool, but don't try to be too cool.

I used to hear this kind of advice and feel really hurt. Why was I hearing I had to act a certain way? I was escaping from hell! Obviously you have been hurt and you want the court to help you. Your abuser will have plenty of books to read about getting his rights in court, so you do the same thing. Remember: you have the right to be angry or to feel numb and crazy, but if you act like that, you'll have trouble getting the judge's sympathy and the custody of your kids.

Try to have a support person from a shelter or a friend or a lawyer with you if you need to appear in court. And take along an invisible hug from me. If you have children, ask for emergency custody orders as well as a restraining order to keep him away from you. If you can, get to a shelter (more on that in the next chapter). If you don't think he'll come after you to hurt you or you can afford a security system, consider staying at home where you are, and getting him thrown out. That sounds pretty cold, I know, but remember: once you decide to leave, you want to know your options. You'll have trouble sorting through lots of ideas and advice, so I'm giving you an idea of the choices you may want to make.

Now you see why the section started with spiritual survival? Don't feel overwhelmed by all this information. Remember, knowledge is power!

Ask the police to escort you and the children, if you have them, to safety. *If they refuse to arrest the batterer, get their names and badge numbers.* Spend the night in the police station if you must, and report them to their commanding officer. Now, the police may try to arrest *you* if you fought back, or even if you called 911 and then he says *you* hit *him.* Don't be surprised if your batterer does this. It happens all the time. One friend of mine, a tiny woman, called 911 when her huge hulking boyfriend hit her. He tried to get her arrested, and the police told her that if she insisted they would arrest him, but they would have to arrest her, too. Ludicrous! Absolute nonsense! It happens. It happened to me once, long ago.

Please don't let this information scare you into not reaching out. So many books I read had that effect on me. I just don't want you to feel, if it happens to you, that you're being struck by lightning. It's just that the system still needs to wake up to domestic violence. But things *are* improving, so gather your resources, go to battered women's support groups, get shelter phone numbers, call hotlines, *and call 911 if he hits you!*

If you are seriously thinking of killing him, just remember one thing: he is not worth the trouble. Don't do it. *Get a protective order, move away, hide, hold a press conference, take out an ad in the local paper, do whatever you must do to protect yourself, but do not kill him.* In spite of all that is said in the press about the "battered woman defense," it's still a pretty iffy proposition and you might do some serious time in jail even if you aren't convicted of first-degree murder. Besides, there are ways of getting free.

Your whole strategy is to stay safe, stay alive, get into recovery, and grow your way out of all of this pain. Don't try to hurt him by sleeping with his friends, slashing his clothes, burning his car, or carrying out any of the other crazy ideas people get when they are hurt. Don't try to have him fired.

I see women obsessed with "trying to protect" other people from the abuser. Well, you heard it here first: you'll look like an idiot or worse if you do that. Let the abuser keep his job, get remarried, and be happy. Stay in your own center of peace and healing and just get on with your own life. I see women ending up looking and sounding like Glenn Close in *Fatal Attraction,* and it even turns me off. *Let go!* I don't think most of us will end up going nuts in the process of getting out of a sick relationship, but I do want to caution you.

If he violates the order of protection, go back to court or insist he be arrested. Get an appointment with someone at the district attorney's office—go with a friend if you can—and ask why he hasn't been arrested for violating the order. *Fight.*

Maybe it will seems that you're the only one who cares, but you must make the system work to protect you. *Get a permanent restraining order if he does not give up and you're still frightened of him.* One attorney told me it can be hard to get a permanent order. Why? "Judges don't want to issue orders that can have a person arrested." The women in the group he was speaking to went ballistic. A judge said, "Well, I understand: we don't want to have the guy arrested if we don't believe he's dangerous." I piped up, ever the irritating law student, and said, "But he'll only be arrested if he violates the order, right? Your Honor?" Hmm . . . they kind of understood it when they saw it from that point of view!

It may seem harsh to have him arrested, but it is much more cruel for him to abuse the person he says he loves, and arrest may be a wake-up call for him. It may push him into a treatment program. It may make you safe. *Whether or not you get him arrested, though, you may end up in family court.* But we'll go over civil court quickly so you can benefit from changes in the law.

Many states have made domestic violence and stalking a "tort." Wonderful, but what's a tort? Is it a chocolate cake? No, that's a torte. A tort is a "civil wrong." (Many torts are also crimes.) This means you can sue a person for hurting you, especially if he does so intentionally—meaning that he knew he was doing it, and it was likely to cause you harm. You can often get payment of medical and psychological costs, and may even get punitive costs—to punish him, and to stop others from doing the same thing.

In community property states, where they give him half of your house even if he did beat you nearly to death, *these new laws can help you keep everything.* Ask your lawyer if such laws apply. Civil court can help you to stop a stalker: if he has any money or a job or a car, you might be able to file a suit for stalking, and he might just figure out that he will have to pay you for his obsession. Nothing cools a person off quite like the idea of losing money. Again, you'll have to talk to a lawyer about this, but I predict that family lawyers will be doing some lawsuits, or personal injury lawyers will be doing divorce work. These new laws can help protect you and your children, though they probably will only work if he has money. If you have money and just want to be sure he stops stalking you, try suing him just to get rid of him. Isn't the law grand?

Family court sessions are often held in civil courthouses. Sometimes, juvenile cases and cases to do with trusts, wills, and other family-related matters are heard in family court. Family law is different from state to state, so here are some key issues to discuss with your lawyer, if you don't know from a friend or family member who has been through the divorce process recently in your state.

Is your state a community property state? If so, the money in the bank account, the house, and most family businesses might be half yours and half his. Of course, he may have put title to the house in his name, but a good lawyer can often prove it is really "community property." And if he has hurt you during the marriage (we are not talking broken heart, but bruises, cuts, threats, terror), see the section above, about torts, for getting your fair share of your community property.

Is your state an equitable distribution state? If so, the home often goes to the mother of the children. (This can happen in community property states, too.)

But more important, perhaps, is this: *Does your state have joint custody?* Joint child custody states are often very hard for abused women, since custody battles can be very expensive, and batterers often appear very smooth and slick. A judge may even award custody to the batterer. That is the bad news. It can happen. The good news is that you can usually insist that the record of domestic violence be accepted and examined by the judge, even if he or she doesn't want to hear about it. Then if the judge ignores the abuse, you can appeal the decision or try to get another judge to hear the case again. The problem is that custody cases are expensive, and you probably don't have much money.

If the judge orders evaluations done to see who is the best parent, try to be sure the evaluator is experienced in domestic violence cases. Ask shelters whom they recommend, or whom they say to avoid. Don't just settle on one because your lawyer "always uses her." The evaluator can make or break your case.

If the evaluation goes against you, try to get a deposition from the evaluator. A deposition is testimony taken out of court. Try to find out how familiar the evaluator is with theories about domestic violence. Is the evaluator biased? Is the evaluator experienced with domestic violence? How many books has he or she read about the subject? How many seminars has this person attended? And so on—you get the picture. It takes a lot of trouble to do a deposition, and costs money, but it could be worth it.

Here I want to make a *suggestion about raising money for legal costs.* Write letters to everyone you know, if necessary, asking for small donations. Some people will be generous and others unkind. I did this once and received many kind letters and donations in various amounts. The people who helped me are treasured in my heart, and if they ever asked me for help, I'd be there for them, too. Sounds kind of desperate, but if you need money for legal fees, it can help to keep this idea in mind.

Custody battles involving child abuse tear families apart. If he did not sexually abuse your children, don't make false allegations! Doing that will work against you; even if allegations are true, they're tough to prove. Do whatever it takes to protect your children. But *don't ever believe that it's a good idea to lie* about that sort of thing, because it's so painful for everyone involved.

But if you do suspect anything, go to your family doctor and ask that the child be examined. Tell the doctor what you think is going on. Perhaps the child will tell the doctor what he or she told you. Then the doctor will have to report it, and you may have medical evidence and the doctor's testimony.

Do whatever it takes to protect your child. You'll never regret it if you do everything it takes. But if you do nothing, your children will continue to be emotionally abused by living in a violent home. Don't be passive. Make plans to get out as soon as you can. Stay away until he gets treatment and stays "recovered." He can prove he is changing by giving you support and help from a distance. You may just decide in the meantime that he has put you through too much to ever deserve a chance with you.

Evidence is important in proving domestic violence. If you go to a doctor with bruises and cuts from the abuse, insist he or she take photos of it. I know you may be in really bad shape when you're in the emergency ward, heaven forbid, but try to be strong and get them to call a shelter or the police or anyone who has a Polaroid camera.

Tell the doctor you were abused and insist he or she write it down. Tell the nurse. Tell everyone. Make sure they write it in your chart and insist on getting your own copy. If anyone tells you the hospital can release your record only to the insurance company or your doctor, threaten to sue them right then and there. You have every right to your own medical records. (I just know the hospitals of America will love me for telling you this.)

Attach copies of the medical report and any photos to the affidavit so they become part of the court record. If you can, get affidavits from friends or family who have seen him hurt you. This may be impossible, but you can ask if you have time. Put in everything you have to convince the judge that you are in fear of your life, or that he has threatened to hurt you if you go to the authorities.

There are books to help you understand the court system in your state. That's the final "mini-lesson" of this chapter: *how to find resources.* Go to the courthouse and get any pamphlets they have on family court proceedings. Read them, try to understand them. See if you can get blank court forms to get familiar with them.

Try your local library to find books about divorce and read them there if you feel uncomfortable about reading them at home. If you have children but are not married, you might still need help: advice on what a deposition or "discovery" is, what to expect in a custody dispute.

Legal Aid (or whatever the organization that provides poor people with lawyers is called in your state) may help you, but may not be available to help you in "contested divorces." Some lawyers work on a "sliding scale," meaning they charge lower fees to people with lower incomes, but you want to get the best lawyer you can afford.

Some law schools (not many) have clinics for abused women. In large cities, many women's groups have formed legal services organizations specializing in battered women's needs. Call local law schools (they'll love me for suggesting this) or ask your local shelter.

New York City has several very fine advocacy groups that can refer you to private lawyers who have been trained in these kinds of cases. And they can help you fill out your forms. One group, for which I worked, is the Center for Battered Women's Legal Services in Manhattan.

If the abuser kidnaps your child, call the police and make a report. Call the FBI if you think he has gone to a foreign country. Some countries have agreements with the United States about returning kidnapped children, but it is a federal crime to steal your own child and take him or her abroad—unless you're fleeing domestic violence. (*Don't kidnap the child yourself;* you'll still risk losing the child and/or going to jail.)

Leaving the state with the child is also a risky thing to do. You could end up in jail or losing custody. There is usually a better way to stay safe. Running and hiding is expensive, difficult, and often illegal. It is so hard on the children and on you. My heart is with you. Don't let any of this scare you. Like everything else in this book, it is only meant to give you the building blocks to create your own place of safety.

I lost custody of my own children to my abuser in part because I left California and went to Oregon. You risk losing custody of your children if you take them to another state without permission. Even if you really believe he will hurt you or your kids unless you leave, remember that risk. Until the laws change, you have to work within the rules as they are. *Try hard to do so,* even if you hear lots of horror stories about it. It's still better than going back to the abuser.

By the way, when discussing the children with police, the court, your lawyer, or friends, always refer to them as "our children" or "the children," not "my children."

Finally, how do you find an attorney who will work for you and your case? The fact is lawyers are expensive, but you will want to get the best you can afford. You will want to be sure he or she is good at domestic violence cases so that you don't have to pay for him or her to learn about it! Also, sometimes you can get some good assistance at a legal clinic, or through Legal Aid, or at courthouses.

To launch your search:

1. FOCUS: You are looking for an attorney who has the same beliefs you do. He or she *must* believe in what you are fighting for (probably your children). Don't hire an unethical sleaze because you think he is going to play mean and dirty. That decision will probably come back to haunt you. But a clever lawyer is okay.

2. GET A LIST OF ATTORNEYS: Your friends and relatives will offer their list (do not necessarily weigh their advice too heavily). Focus on getting names from people who deal with these issues continually: workers at shelters and counseling offices; other attorneys; church people. You need about thirty names before you start calling.

3. CALL ALL THE LAWYERS: Leave a message and then wait until they call you back. (Some never will.)

4. INTERVIEW THE LAWYERS: Here are some questions to ask:

- "How many cases are you handling at one time?"

- "How many do you have going right now?"

- "How is your office organized?"
  You want to know how many research assistants the lawyer has, and how many paralegals. In this context, there are no right answers. Part of what you are looking for is how the lawyer reacts to your asking these questions.
  Your best bet is not necessarily the most charming lawyer, nor the most sympathetic. You want someone you can work with, and who you feel you can trust. When you visit the office, assess how clean and organized it is. The most beautiful office is not necessarily the best. You simply want someone who's reasonably together.

- "How quickly will you usually return my calls?"

- "Who will be calling me back: the attorney, a paralegal, a legal secretary, a law clerk?"

- "Will the attorney give me a referral? That is, can I call one of his previous clients?"

- "How knowledgeable is the attorney about domestic violence?"

- "How many cases has he worked on?"

- "How many years of experience, and what background, does the lawyer have? What kinds of cases has he or she handled?"

- "What are the costs, fees, monthly payment plans?"
  Also, the "family law specialist" tag does not always give you the best attorney.

- "Can I observe the attorney in court?"
  If the answer is negative, beware.

There is no magic formula for finding the best lawyer for your case. However, always remember that it is *your* case. These questions should be of help to you in making your selection.

Try to make monthly payments to your attorney. Many lawyers complain that their clients have cable TV, go out to restaurants and movies, but can't seem to pay even a small amount on their legal bill. You can't expect a lawyer to work for nothing.

Finally, keep copies of all your documents and keep your own files tidy.

Avoid calling your attorney except to discuss the case. Attorneys get too many calls unrelated to the legal aspects of the case.

Make use of your support system (counselors, friends, family, hotlines) if you are worried.

Staying Sane in a Shelter

During the 1980s I lived in Iran, with visits back to my family in California. From 1985 to 1987 my marriage became more violent. After I had been in Iran for two years, I was able to leave with our two sons, one of whom had been born in Tehran. Two years was longer than any of our previous stays in Iran. In that time, not only was my husband physically and emotionally abusive, but he sold our home in New York; he would not let me leave Iran until all the funds from the sale had been sent to him.

The first phone call I made from my parents' home in Laguna Beach, California, was to a women's shelter that had just opened, Human Options. This was the first I learned about shelters and support groups. My husband came over to visit and threaten us. And I became pregnant with our third son. It took one more pregnancy and a lot of counseling, prayer, and fear before I finally went to a shelter with my children.

What I have learned since about domestic violence and the battered-woman syndrome was not as important to me as what I learned by staying in shelters with my children. I will try to share with you this knowledge, which I paid a real price to get: *how to tell if you need a shelter, how to find one, and what to do when you are there.*

If you are the person who is living in pain in an abusive relationship, only you can make the choice to leave. Maybe you don't need a shelter. Gauge the danger by using the "thermometer" chart in Letter 1, and follow the advice of your support group, starting with your own inner voice of sanity. But first, some advice and observations. Pick through this, remembering that it's just my own personal view and should not be any more important than what you find out on your own. You may have a different idea or feel strongly one way or another.

It's very important to have the phone number of a hotline.

Equally important, get *the numbers of shelters and women's groups* from the yellow pages or from Directory Assistance. Some advocates leave cards with phone numbers in women's bathrooms at restaurants and gas stations. I think it would be great if restaurants and gas stations offered to keep brochures in their ladies' rest rooms so women could read about shelters in their own private place.

You can often get a local number by calling **1-800-799-SAFE,** a toll-free number set up by the federal government when President Clinton and Congress put into law the Violence Against Women Act (VAWA). Sometimes police stations, YWCAs, women's clubs, and churches (not often enough!) have information about shelters. I leave it to you to find the number you need. Look in your phone book, call the 800 number, find your local hotline.

After you are safe, in a good solid place, turn around and make sure your church offers this information. Promise me and yourself you'll do this.

Tell the hotline counselor about your abuse. She can help you assess how bad your situation is.

You may be in danger and not even feel it. I once told Lou Brown my favorite story about why people do things that are, in the end, destructive. The story is, if you drop a frog into a pan of boiling water, it will jump right out. But if you start with cool water and slowly turn up the heat, the frog will die and be boiled because it never noticed the change in temperature. Lou seemed to think this explained quite a few things about violent relationships.

You may not be in a really dangerous, life-threatening situation. Just to be on the safe side ask yourself these questions: Is he is a gun fanatic? Does he have many sharp knives? Has he threatened you with things like "no other man will ever have you if I can't have you"? If these things are true in your situation, then a shelter might be a real necessity.

I beg you to reach out to hotlines and begin to share your story and to do something to protect yourself. If you reach out to your friends and family, they may not believe you. They may have been made a part of the abuser's circle of support without knowing of his abuse of you.

You must build your inner self. Reach out to hotlines because through them you will find connections to support groups and other resources, and to women who have been through your nightmare. They are doing what you will do one day, and that is healing the wounds inside their souls by reaching out to you, with love.

Occasionally you'll get some really bad advice. One woman, who was a law student, gave me some ridiculous advice about how if I did not leave the relationship my abuser could sue me for some strange reason. I mostly got good advice, though, and I mention the law student only to urge you to *test the wisdom of what people are saying,* just as you filter what the abuser says to you and don't give him so much power over you.

Shelters are run by women's groups, the Salvation Army, the YWCA, churches, and other nonprofit groups. Some are very religious in orientation and will insist you pray their way or leave. Others subscribe to varieties of feminism that are anti-man. But if you need a safe place to go with your children, go! If you can find out about different shelters by way of hotlines, try to find one that fit your needs. For example, if you are an Orthodox Jewish woman and need to keep a kosher home for yourself and your children, you will want to find a kosher shelter. They do exist, especially in New York City. If you are lesbian or bisexual, you may be able to find a shelter more appropriate for your needs, though I have never heard of a shelter turning away a lesbian woman with children. Remember, though, there are few places for too many victims; you may need to get on a waiting list or keep calling until you can go there.

Tell the hotline people if you have special needs such as handicaps, or if you need to avoid certain neighborhoods. You don't want to end up in a shelter across the street from your boyfriend's mother's house! Just as we discussed in Letter 3, you'll want to take as much money and documents as you can before leaving.

Shelters will not give out their addresses. They may not take boys over a certain age, since teenage boys can get violent with other children. This is one reason I encourage you to get out while they are still young, as tough as it is to handle youngsters on your own.

If the police have been called and they will take you to a shelter, or to the police station to get a ride to a shelter, ask them to restrain the abuser while you *get your stash of documents*. One member of my support network suggested having a notebook or folder with pockets and keeping copies of bank statements, deeds, car registrations, and keys. I say, *take the originals of all deeds and registrations belonging to you,* photocopy everything else you can, and hide your stash (the "getaway kit") in a safe place—with a friend who is completely trustworthy, with your lawyer, or in some safe place he'll never look. Only you can know where that is, but be careful, you don't want to tip him off.

Some shelters have great programs that offer day care, long-term shelter, referrals to counseling, and help getting social services like Aid to Families with Dependent Children, food stamps, and so on. *Don't be ashamed of needing help.* One day you will be on the other end, giving back. Life is like that. Reach out to the help offered and, if necessary, demand it. Your children and you do not deserve this abuse. Get out and get safe.

Your children may feel really safe in the shelter, and they may just be so glad you are safe that they adjust quickly to life there. Once they feel safe they may tell you things you had no idea of. Maybe their daddy beat them, too. Maybe he sexually abused them. Sexual abuse is hard to prove, but if your children tell you it happened, tell a staff person at the shelter, and see what you can do to protect them.

You'll need a great deal of support, and you may feel you are going insane. Move slowly through this pain; things will not be "right" for a while. Take great comfort in knowing that you are out of that relationship, and that you will not go back to that one or any other like it.

Younger children take to life in shelters more easily than the older ones. It is harder for older children, who may miss their toys and special clothes. Try to take some of their favorite things, if you can. Often shelters have a stash of toys for kids, but I found one shelter where you practically had to beg to get a box of crayons for them! It's weird, isn't it? Many of the people running shelters don't even have children, and I just love it when social workers who don't have kids tell you how to parent. Take their advice, try to follow it, learn new ways of parenting.

Not to be negative, but you may want to get a TB (tuberculosis) test when you enter the shelter, and follow up after you leave, or a few months later. While the odds are not high that you will be exposed to TB in a shelter, the illness is epidemic among homeless people in America. If you are exposed, you can avoid a bad case of TB by getting treatment early. I got TB in a shelter. (Why do I have to tell you all these terrible things.) I hope that won't make you afraid to get into a shelter. Do, though, get a TB test to avoid what I went through six years later, when my TB went "active." (I'm okay now.)

Shelters need the support of the communities they are in. They need church volunteers to bring platters of lasagna and companionship for the families in shelters. They need, among other things, donations of disposable diapers, new and used toys, furniture, clothing, pots, pans, and—this is something many women's groups do—small grooming kits of shampoo and toothbrushes and so forth. One day you will look back and reach out to help shelters with donations of money, cans of tuna, boxes of paper towels, and other stuff. For now, you're on the receiving end; remind yourself, every time you feel ashamed, that *it is more blessed to give than to receive, and so you are helping the person helping you receive a great blessing.* You need not be ashamed that you are in a shelter. *You are on your way to recovery, safety, and serenity. Congratulations!*

So you have a support network of people who know about domestic violence, and they have encouraged you to get into a shelter. Maybe you feel you're better off staying at home and getting a restraining order to keep him away from you and get him out of the house. You have made a few preparations, such as getting your birth certificates and Social Security cards, and you may even have a bit of money saved to tide you over. You have called hotlines and have found a shelter which suits your needs.

I know how terrified you are. You are afraid he will hurt or even kill you. But, by staying for fear of the unknown, you are condemning yourself to a prison that will destroy your spirit. When I look back on my days of fear and being a prisoner to an abusive husband, I feel great compassion for myself. I forgive myself for staying with him. Because of the relationship, I have three beautiful children. My fear was always that he would kidnap them and take them to Iran. Guess what? He did it, and I survived it. My children suffer from not knowing their mother, and by growing up away from their American side, but they are taken care of, well fed, and taken to doctors; I have completed a good education and hope one day to have them back in my life. But the point is, even at the cost of losing my dear sons, it was worth it to leave a very painful relationship. Now that I have a bachelor's degree, a master's degree, and a law degree, I can giggle at how he used to call me stupid. It seems like such a long time ago, and very far away. You will look back and wonder why you stayed, but you will remember, too, your great courage in stepping into freedom, either by going to a shelter or by getting that restraining order.

While you live in the shelter, you will have to follow its rules. Often the rules are very different from shelter to shelter. *Shelters are not perfect places, but do not try to fix them!* Get yourself on your feet; try to meet other survivors who are a little further along in their recovery from abuse than you are. You may meet some pretty messed-up people in shelters. You may meet women who are shattered beyond repair. I met some very fine women in the shelters in Portland, whose memory I cherish. I hope to meet them again. Some were residents of the shelter; others were staff members. I met some real weirdos, too—but, you know, life is like that.

Go through the intake process, fill out the forms, ask for help, take whatever help you can get.

Get your children registered in school.

Get your restraining order and have it served on the abuser.

Appear in court with an escort if the court or shelter provides it. If you are concerned about security, call the courthouse and ask for a bailiff to meet you at the front door; then arrive by taxi, so you can drive up and walk in. If the courthouse doesn't have a metal detector, you can even ask to have the abuser searched if he appears. I admit, these may seem extreme measures, but if they make you feel safe and you are terrified, well, just go ahead and ask for all the help you can get.

You may not be able to safely return to your job. You may need to be on welfare for a while, which is very hard. But don't let fear of that stop you from getting to safety.

Remember to take all these thoughts as a starting point for your own recovery. They are less important than what you already know, and that is that you deserve a life free of threats and free of verbal abuse. You deserve to live a violence-free life, especially in your own home!

Don't worry about what will happen to your boyfriend or husband after you leave. He may promise to change—and you know what? There are many great programs to help men learn how not to batter women. Many batterers just kind of fall apart when their women leave them. That's also exactly what they need to go through to get themselves well mentally. *Only when they hit bottom have they gotten where they need to get if they're to turn their lives around.*

Your man may just disappear, or he may fight to get you back, or he may get really abusive and try to get custody of your kids, or have you go through some horrible court battle. I have seen all of that.

But freedom is worth it. And success is what you do with your life after you leave the bondage of these relationships.

Now, on to the Promised Land.

Staying Safe
- - - - - - - - - - - - - - - - - - - -

This may scare you into staying in your abusive relationship, if you haven't left already. Don't let it do that. I used to read books about domestic violence and I'd get so scared of leaving, I'd stop planning to get out.

Look, the odds are you will not die of domestic violence if you leave. Leaving will be a dangerous time, and you will need to take precautions, but you can and will do your best to stay alive.

Don't let these words scare you. It is silly to stay in a situation that is getting progressively worse and worse. You can create your own support system, find your inner strength, make plans for the getaway, and either get to a shelter or get an order keeping him away from you.

So now you're out of the relationship. But he keeps calling you, sending you letters, telling you through friends and family that he "still loves you." If he is not working really hard with a batterers' group to get retrained, don't even think about going back to him. *He will abuse you again.*

Even very religious shelters that operate on the basis that marriage is a sacred commitment to God will insist that their residents not go back until the batterer has been in treatment for many, many months. Just following that advice can keep you safe.

If you are strong enough to say no to the abuser and you don't cave in and go back to him, you must *take precautions.*

Have a restraining order, and keep a copy with you. Be sure your local police station has a copy of it. Go in there and talk to an officer and get his or her card. *Leave a copy of your restraining order with the officer, and go in another day to make sure he or she has it.*

Getting your copy of the order from the court to the police station can be difficult, because frequently the police refuse to accept the order. But this is where your local legal aid office or courthouse can help. If you can't get it done, call a lawyer specializing in domestic violence and ask what resources are out there. I personally believe the legal system needs to establish clinics for domestic violence in every county in America. Until that day, you'll have to use what is out there to get that restraining order into your hands and into the hands of other people who need it.

If you're getting an apartment, try to rent one with some security. Tell the security staff and your neighbors about your situation. Don't go into gory details, just show them photos of the abuser and tell them to call 911 if they see him around.

At this point, you need to have a two-minute version of your story to tell people so you don't overwhelm them. If they want to know more about your abuse or abuse in general, suggest they read this book. I know it sounds like we are endlessly telling you to help us distribute this book, but books can help explain things too painful and complex to talk about. *Not Without My Daughter,* by Betty Mahmoodi, helped "explain" my situation. I knew her in Iran (I am the "diabetic" in her book). I thank God she had the courage to tell her story, because it makes mine easier to tell.

A short version of your story will save time and keep you private as well as safe. Talk about your history. If you meet people who challenge the truth of your story, at least you know who to avoid.

Say you have your restraining order, you have a safe place to live, and the abuser won't give up. *Drag him back to court or sue him for stalking you.* Stand on the roof and scream at the world if no one will help you. Go to the local papers if the police refuse to arrest the stalker. Be noisy. The squeaky wheel not only gets the grease, it also keeps on turning. So raise the stakes for the abuser. If you must, get an unlisted phone number, change jobs, sue him, try to get him arrested, but only in response to his attempt to hurt you, stalk you, or get you back into the relationship with him.

Don't try to get him fired from his job, and don't try to "protect" others (other women, for instance) from him. If he gets a new wife or girlfriend, only warn her if she asks. Remember, you are responsible only for you. Women often get off track in trying to destroy the abuser. This is a big mistake. Keep your focus on yourself.

Do not hire a hit man. Sounds crazy to mention it, but all of us, I assure you, have had the idea. In many ways, we have been with the same guy and been through the same painful experiences. Some are worse than others. But wanting to kill someone is just a bad thought; as long as you take no action and make no plans to do it, especially with another person, it is not a crime. You may want to keep from telling your therapist about this. I told one therapist I was so upset I wanted to see my abuser dead, and she reported me to the police. They laughed at her, and I got another therapist.

I no longer want to see my ex-husband suffer. I only want to see my children again, and I hope for the best for all of us. I wish my own nightmare would finally wind down, but I know many people face more immediate concerns. How can they avoid more abuse by the person they have escaped from once?

There are lots of new laws concerning violence against women, and many people, also known as lawyers, don't know the first thing about these laws. Ask the police what laws apply to your situation. Ask your shelter. Find ways of staying safe. We can learn more about the new laws and insist that the police and district attorneys use them to protect us.

If you can't get anyone to help you, be creative. Think calmly about the problem. Is he a danger to you or your children? Do you have a restraining order? *If he violates the order even once, call the police and report it. Call them again and report new violations. Get a record of your reports from the police, take them to the district attorney, and ask why he won't prosecute the abuser.*

Many women believe their abuser is so wild that if they get a restraining order he will go off and buy a weapon. Maybe so. Often, instead, the abuser will get scared of authority and leave you alone. You must try to figure out what you are dealing with here. If he has a good job or is even kind of semi-employed, he is more stable. This makes it harder to "prove" to a jury or judge that he's the nightmare you say he is, but it gives you an advantage. He may not want to deal with a prosecution or a civil lawsuit. You can sue him if he insists on stalking you, and while it may cost you time and money to do it, it might be enough to get him to go away.

The most important tool or weapon you have is your own attitude and belief that you have the right to live free from violence. You have the right to keep this person away from you. Don't let anyone tell you anything different. If he won't leave you alone, use a combination of therapy, legal assistance, and evasive tactics. Change your pattern of commuting to work. Get a post office box and *get a cellular phone* instead of having a listed or unlisted phone number. Keep one phone with an answering machine and get another phone line for your regular calls. This way, if he keeps calling (he's not apt to suspect a second phone number), you can keep a tape of his calls and your friends' messages won't be mixed with his.

Some men are absolute monsters, but yours most likely will not end up being one. Chances are, he will go away and find a new victim. It is not your problem if he does. Get on with your own path. Leaving him in the dust and insisting on your own safety will save your life. Get involved with the shelter movement; raise money for shelters; be a public speaker; make sure your local police department and DA's office have education programs on domestic violence. Go to local law schools and ask if they have such programs. You may want to offer to speak to those classes.

Law schools are mostly nonprofit and get tax breaks from the state and federal government. If they fail to teach basic skills to new lawyers, we will not see much in the way of improvement in the legal system. I don't think there's a lot in that last sentence any of my professors would approve of, but it says a lot about how I feel about law schools and domestic violence.

I don't exactly know how else to tell you to stay safe. You must reach out to your own resources and stay strong. *Be a squeaky wheel.* Fight for others as well as yourself. Together we can change things.

Beginning Your Recovery

Recovery from a battering relationship is a long, slow journey with lots of wonderful surprises along the way. Some of the things you will learn and experience may be frightening, but your strength will grow as long as you learn to protect yourself—not only from the person who hurt you, but also from some problems many of us have faced.

One important thing you'll need is *a support system.* Whether or not you are in a shelter, try to connect with a group of other women who have gone through an abusive relationship. Sometimes shelters or women's groups offer support groups for women in recovery from such relationships. You can try to start your own if you can't find one. Ask first at shelters and get referrals to other sources of group help.

One-on-one therapy is a really good thing, but here is the first warning of this topic: *be very careful about your therapist.* There are some really bad therapists (and other professionals) out there. You want to be sure your therapist has a lot of experience working with battered women. Keep looking until you find one.

Let me share with you some missteps and good experiences from my own personal files.

I had a series of therapists I'd meet with on trips to America from Iran who had absolutely no clue about why I was in this really bad relationship. I hinted at threats to kidnap my children and they'd say, "You need to talk to a lawyer; it's a legal problem." Well, the lawyers at that point told me there wasn't much I could do, and I'd need therapy to get strength to leave the relationship. Back to the therapist. Back to the relationship. I felt no one understood my fears.

My most memorable visit to a therapist took place when the "addictive relationship" theory was popular. I was trying to tell this gal what my fears were and how I wanted to get safe and away from my abuser, and she told me, "You're an addict." Well, thanks. I don't think I needed that.

Psychologists had told me that I wasn't strong-willed enough, too strong-willed, not brave enough, too willing to take risks, abused as a child, abused as an adult, and so on. In other words, I'd been labeled with every kind of psychobabble coming down the pike. Now, according to this therapist, I was an addict. Great!

Well, I read every self-help book there was and got lots of ideas from them, but mainly *I was an injured person looking for support.* I sought legal help, psychological help, therapy for my children, family support, you name it. I really needed some help planning my escape from the relationship, and no one seemed to be able to help me sit down and lay out the problems I had and come up with some solutions to them. I dearly loved the members of my group therapy and the various people who tried to help me, but what I really needed was what I am trying to help you find: a method of planning.

You must realize that you are responsible. Don't throw this book across the room. I don't mean that you hurt yourself or that you wanted this pain. *Responsible* means *capable of responding* (this is from Lisa, a member of my New York support group). That's all. You must begin to use feelings and thoughts you have had to hide for fear of getting more abuse thrown at you. You need some therapy and support so you can do that safely.

I hid much of my agony for years after I lost my children. I would begin therapy when I felt so depressed I could not even work, and then some "quick save" would arrive and I'd quit. I did have trouble finding good therapists and affording them, but I recommend you get help however you can get it. *It's dangerous to go this alone,* as I did.

My quick saves included stressful jobs, entry into demanding educational plans, moves across the country, and relationships that were lovely yet did not fill that inner need for healing. After a really crippling depression finally turned into false-memory syndrome (I thought I had been abused as a child; I filled in the details and two therapists totally "believed" me; I broke down, then found a therapist who slowly, patiently walked me through these scary memories until we discovered they were not really based in fact), I found some therapy with a person who saved my life.

My therapist was an angel. *She mostly listened to me.* Week after week I'd drag myself to her office in uptown Manhattan, talk almost nonstop, and leave slightly unburdened. She remembered things I had said and put them together for me weeks later with a sentence or two. I found insights. I pieced myself together. My shattered spirit and psyche healed. My depression was so crippling at the time that I stay in therapy to avoid ever slipping into such a state. If it begins again, I will likely take medication to avoid that sinking spiral.

Mine is an extreme example, because my former husband kidnapped our children and took them to Iran; every few years I'd get a message that one of our sons needed brain surgery, and it was my fault if he died. These were lies, but I had no way of knowing that. My abuse continues as I write this, but the therapy and the hard work I have put into my recovery will, I hope, help you in yours. Your experience will, I pray, be easier. Chances are, at the very least, the abuse will end.

One thing I find in myself as well as others is that the abuser can still push our buttons. *Learn what your hot buttons are and disconnect them!* For example, if he knows he can make you feel bad by telling you you're a failure, be sure you filter that message. Who is he to tell you what you are? Nobody. He has no power over you, unless you give it to him.

Get your financial independence as quickly as possible. I know how hard this is. If you have young children or even older ones, money will be a big struggle. Even women alone with no children struggle. Welfare can be a necessary first step. Try quickly to get day care and a job, apply for school, get a plan together. *Most women who get welfare* (officially, Aid to Families with Dependent Children, AFDC) *stay on it for a short time.* Don't think that if you get welfare you'll be stuck, and your children's children will be on it. This is a frightening myth. The truth is that AFDC can be an essential stepping-stone for you.

This book cannot provide all the answers to any part of your recovery. It is only meant to *guide* you in finding your own answers. I can tell you what I did, and what others did, and how you can plan your own road map. Remember that *I don't expect you to do it my way or anyone else's way. Your way will be an inspiration for other women.* The worst of circumstances can be turned around and bring about the deepest and most important experiences in our lives. Yes, they are the most painful—but they also often prove to be the most helpful. I only expect that after you have found your path, you will help others like yourself. Survivors of violence are the best source of ongoing recovery in America. We carry the light and we can help others light their candles. Together we will banish the shadows and fears.

I had to find a job right after I lost my children. They were gone to Iran and I was broke, utterly broke. I had purchased a second-hand computer with the guidance of a very smart friend who also helped me learn how to use it.

I already knew how to type. If you know how to type, you can get a job. You can learn to use a computer program. There are word-processing classes and programs in nearly every community; if you can do so, get this training. You may want to apply for unemployment or other assistance to help you to get through the next few months. No job skills usually means no job. But if you sew, perhaps you can do alterations or make things to sell. If you're good with children, perhaps you can baby-sit. Sit down and write out what you know how to do, and what you like to do. It seems kind of dumb, but writing things down really is a first step to finding your path to recovery.

I got temporary jobs in law firms and corporations. I was still in such pain I could barely function, but I loved being in the corporate kind of office and was excited to learn new skills. Voice mail, for example, was a mystery to me. I was very friendly to people but had no clue as to what was expected of me. I did my best but found I was underemployed and unable to fit into the secretarial mold.

I moved to New York. It was kind of crazy to do that, since I knew no one, but I had computer skills and a clear idea of the kind of job I wanted. I had a salary in mind and a résumé all prepared, and I knew New York would offer me the opportunity to get an education.

I found a job my first day there, and after staying with a dear relative in New Jersey, got an apartment with a view of Manhattan. I had a lovely landlady, and I felt the excitement of a new city and a new life. It helped me avoid my pain from the kidnapping and the years of abuse. I soon got a better job in a law firm, one filled with some of the best people I have ever had the pleasure of knowing. The secretaries, paralegals, and lawyers, even the security guards and telephone operators, were such fine people that I felt deeply blessed, though I worked way too hard. I still cherish my boss, who encouraged me in my pursuit of a law degree. He remains part of my support system. I often think of him and the words of encouragement and advice he gave me; the memory feeds my own continuing recovery.

Others may think, "Well, she just lucked out and met good people." I have news for you: *most people are good people.* They have some core of kindness. You need to sift out the vampires and the negative people—that is, the people who doubt you can find your dreams and make them come true. Don't let that stuff come into your soul. Find people who will encourage you, while being careful of wolves in sheep's clothing. Realize, too, that good people sometimes give you bad advice. Filter it all out and you will find your own wisdom for your own life.

It can be very easy to be a victim again. Employers will overwork you and underpay you. If that happens, find a new job. "Oh," you say, "jobs are hard to find." Don't let that stop you. A job is only a job. Figure out what you hate about the job, and if you can't fix it, get a résumé out there and find your way into a new place.

You must get an education. You can get a general equivalency diploma (GED) if you have no high school diploma. You can even get a college degree this way. I did. My college degree (a bachelor of science in liberal arts) comes from the Regents College Degrees Program in Albany, New York. Look for programs funded by states and local governments to get your college degree a little faster than usual. Look for ways to get credit for life experience and for tests that earn you credit; there are other programs, too, which many colleges kind of keep a secret. Remember, you must *ask questions* and be willing to go to a library and look for books to tell you how to do what you want to do.

Lots of people will tell you they did fine with no education.

Maybe so. Maybe you will be one of those people. I happen to treasure my education because now I see and understand things that I couldn't see or understand before. But even if plenty of people can live without education, I just wonder why we should keep from learning. Learning keeps us young, cute, happy, and sexy. Well, okay, maybe none of the above is true, but education can't hurt, can it?

When I tell people about these programs, it takes me about twenty minutes to get through their suspicions: "I've never heard of that." "Sounds too good to be true." "Do you know anyone who has done that?" This is after I've told them five times, "I did this." So just decide to get your education no matter what the cost.

There are loan programs and scholarships. There are work-study programs, and you can live with roommates or in housing on college campuses. But you will get there only if you decide, "I will get my education." *Write it down.*

Go to local campuses. Go to the local library and ask your librarian for books on getting a degree. There is an old Persian saying, "If you want to be a professor, ask in a hundred places, and cut in one place." You must get out there and ask questions. I know it can be done.

I got my bachelor's degree and was then accepted into a graduate program at New York University. It may be impossible for you to do that—I'll admit I was fortunate and blessed—but you must work to create opportunities. You must fill out application forms, set goals, talk to people, and work hard to create choices for yourself down the road.

Law school was kind of the same way. I had finished my master's thesis for NYU and felt I had to leave New York, so I went back to Oregon to take the Law School Admissions Test, the LSAT. This was the ultimate "geographic" fix. Therapy would have been cheaper and easier, but what the heck. I went to Oregon, took the

LSAT, applied for school in Portland, and was accepted. But I was too depressed and overwhelmed. I returned to New York and stayed with a dear friend, who graciously saw me through a true emotional meltdown.

Incredibly, in the middle of all this, I got an invitation in the mail to start classes at a New York school, Cardozo—the next week.

Not that many of you will be faced with this problem, but if you are, I hope you get a good therapist before embarking on law school. Even if you aren't in the situation I was in (I'm diabetic; I had some physical problems that made the diabetes worse, my three sons were in Iran . . .), survivors of violence will have a really hard time in law school. Everyone has a hard time; it will be a little worse for you.

Law school in America is a bit like marine boot camp for the brain and emotions. You come out a little worse for wear, but transformed into this analytical person who speaks confidently about things even when you really know they're not exactly set in stone. You take a position and attack the other person's. If you can't do it well enough, you will suffer. Law school is obviously not the solution for most of us. I do not want you to think you have to go. I figure I'll tell you how I did it, and maybe you'll think if Merritt did it, I can work out my own path to my own goals.

(I did find that the way lawyers are taught about domestic violence is just about as primitive and idiotic as possible. Most of us are taught about battered women who are accused of murdering their batterers. Well, get a clue, law schools of America: domestic violence is a plague that is infecting our nation, killing women, crippling children emotionally and physically, and the legal system is about the only way out for victims!)

If you are struggling to get your lawyer or a prosecutor to do something, be sure he or she has read this book. Buy it for him or her if you must. Tell your local shelter to insist that police officers get training in how to handle domestic violence, or at least read this book. We have kept it short for "regular people who want to know more" and for you, the victim/survivor. There is no excuse for people not to know about the traps women face in leaving violent relationships.

That's enough of Merritt on the soapbox. But if you want to know why lawyers, judges (99 percent of whom used to be lawyers), and prosecutors are so clueless, remember, most people who go through law school in America, even today, are not trained in domestic violence.

Your recovery will depend on your ability to get a support group together (even if it is a once-every-two-week meeting or a matter of having friends, therapists, and other people who encourage you), and on restoring your shattered self-image and spirit. Please learn from my mistakes and *don't wait too long to get help.* The results, like a crippling depression, can cost you your savings account, your job, your friends, and all you have in your life. Get help, and look for therapists as carefully as you look for lawyers. Ask in a hundred places, and make a good choice.

Be willing to change therapists if yours turns out badly. One therapist I had, a man, stepped over the boundary line and actually discussed his dating and sex life, telling me he found me attractive. Yuck! I turned him in. I went to the head of the clinic, explained what the therapist said, and asked for my money back. They listened and believed me. They gave me my money back. I moved on to another therapist whom I found through a local women's shelter. She's a sweetheart, much like my New York therapist.

Domestic violence has injured you even if you have no physical scars. Many, many of us have been through it. We stand united in our faith that there is life after the death of a painful relationship. If we can do this, and we have, so can you.

The poem that follows is one I read when I was taking a graduate English course for my master's degree. I believe it says a lot about domestic violence and isolation, about the batterer and his victim. My professor insisted I was wrong, but many women told me after class that they agreed with me. What do you think? I share this with you not because it's a really positive, "up" poem, but because I believe it says a lot about how relationships like these have been worked with in literature. Please let it inspire you to write down your own thoughts and feelings, along with your goals and plans.

Eros Turanos

(Greek for "Love, the Tyrant")

She fears him, and will always ask
What fated her to choose him;
She meets in his engaging mask
All reasons to refuse him;
But what she meets and what she fears
Are less than are the downward years,
Drawn slowly to the foamless weirs
Of age, were she to lose him.

Between a blurred sagacity
That once had power to sound him,
And Love, that will not let him be
The Judas that she found him.
Her pride assuages her almost,
As if it were alone the cost—
He sees that he will not be lost,
And waits and looks around him.

A sense of ocean and old trees
Envelops and allures him;
Tradition, touching all he sees,
Beguiles and reassures him;
And all her doubts of what he says
Are dimmed with what she knows of days—
And fades, and she secures him.

The falling leaf inaugurates
The reign of her confusion;
The pounding wave reverberates
The dirge of her illusion;
And home, where passion lived and died,
Becomes a place where she can hide,
While all the town and harbor side
Vibrate with her seclusion.

We tell you, tapping on our brows,
The story as it should be.—
As if the story of a house
Were told, or ever could be;
We'll have no kindly veil between
Her visions and those we have seen.—
As if we guessed what hers have been,
Or what they are or would be.

Meanwhile we do no harm; for they
That with a god have striven,
Not hearing much of what we say,
Take what the god has given;
Though like waves breaking it may be
Or like a changed familiar tree,
Or like a stairway to the sea
Where down the blind are driven.

—Edwin Arlington Robinson (1916)

Forming New Relationships

Oh, this is great. I am utterly clueless, and can only tell you what I have learned in the hope of helping you recognize your own "Don't do this" or "Well, at least others have made the same mistakes."

I do know that while pain and recovery are threads twisted together in my own life, I love men and I know that almost all of us want to be with someone else.

The problem here is that we have a track record with truly problem guys, who may still be part of our life. We know there are lots of abusive types around us, waiting to be charming and flashy. We can learn from my mistakes.

There are success stories. One recent event in my life that I feel shows I have changed old patterns is hereby shared in all its human idiocy, mostly on my part.

I have a dear friend who, like me, is struggling with the details of her recovery from domestic violence. Her abuser has dragged her through family court with the financial aid of his new wife, who is obviously a sick woman. I mean, this guy not only battered my friend, he batters the new wife, and the new wife has financed a five-figure custody battle. Unbelievable.

But just the other night, listening to some great music at a local café in Laguna, I met this handsome hunk who could have charmed the bark off a tree. We had a spirited discussion and I thought, "Wow, this guy is so adorable." He said he was unmarried and had no children. I hoped to meet him again, but it never quite happened. Then I began to have this nervous feeling: "Why is such a charmer, in such beautiful shape, still single?" I remembered all I know about batterers. Budding lawyer that I am, I analyzed the guy like some kind of mutant virus. I was left with the unsettling feeling that this guy was wearing a mask, and I was quite happy I had avoided the snare.

I visited my buddy and looked through her photo album. Guess who her ex-husband was? Yes, my friends, it was the guy at the café. It's a small world, isn't it? Others might say that maybe God was in this.

People can be abusive emotionally without ever hitting you. Learn to listen to men's tales of past relationships, and you may find you learn "more than you want to know," but exactly what you *need* to know. One key here is, if all his relationships failed because there was something wrong with "her," you may be the next "her" on the list. The other important key is this man's childhood. How does he describe the way his parents related to each other? Did they stay together, or did they get a divorce? Was there alcoholism or other drug abuse? Was there physical or nonphysical abuse? Childhood shapes our entire perspective in relationships.

I suggest that if you date, date men you really don't want to do the horizontal hula with. Really: get to know all kinds of nice guys by having coffee with them or doing social things. You don't have to have romantic relationships. Keep those zippers zipped and you may discover that the guy with all the bells and whistles is keeping his bad temper, his control-freakhood, and his need to be bigger and better than you, all in the closet.

If he wants you to wear a certain kind of perfume, clothing, and so on, be wary. Hey, who died and left this guy in charge of your life? You must go through the process of getting the job and the education and working the program for recovery before you're ready to meet Mr. Right. I think Mr. Right is sort of like Mr. Potato Head: we all know who he is but aren't sure of what he looks like. I say, get a Mr. Potato Head toy and worry about Mr. Right after you have some stability. You may find Mr. Potato Head has some fine qualities.

Okay, I know you'll end up in a relationship and will, according to the statistical odds, get physically intimate with him. I'll only ask you this: If he won't wear a condom, why are you with this idiot? He obviously has no sense of self-preservation, or else he is already infected with the virus that causes AIDS and wants to share it with you. If you are already having sex and not using a condom, get an AIDS test. After leaving the abuser who started you reading this book, get an AIDS test anyway. Follow up with another test six months later.

Did you know there are lots of life-extending treatments for AIDS, though there is no cure? If you are pregnant and you take drugs to fight the virus during the pregnancy, you'll be much less likely to pass the virus to the baby. Hey, I hope you don't face any of this. I hope you are smart, blessed, lucky, whatever. But be real.

Chastity, monogamy, abstinence—these are really the only kinds of safe sex. But condoms are good prevention. I won't trot out my opinions on what you do in your life, any more than I invite any of you into my life in that regard. But knowledge is power. Don't have unsafe sex with anyone. And this is really a good idea if you're with a batterer. Batterers often have sex with all sorts of people— another reason to get away from him.

But the heart of this letter is not to urge you to have safe sex. That is just one vital part of the whole message: that sex or dating or a combination of them leaves you vulnerable to hurt feelings that may overwhelm you. *You may get sucked into a relationship that will become a crutch.*

I know what I'm talking about.

Learn to be healthy and happy on your own or you will attract the invisible walking wounded. They look good, sound good, seem like the perfect diversion, and then *wham.* You're wasting hours on the phone with them and guess what? It won't work because you are both keeping each other from doing that warm and fuzzy work we talked about in the letter on strengthening your inner self.

Well, if I had the key to avoiding bad relationships I'd patent it and sell it. I don't. I know that we know more now than we ever have about how to have a good one. I know that a good relationship starts out the old-fashioned way. Two unhappy halves will not make a happy whole. Find your peace within and you'll be able to spot the snakes, as I did. Find your inner core of happiness, and you won't be dependent on someone else brightening your life. You will be a light, and will learn to keep that candle out of the wind. You'll find people to be with who will be able to tell you when you're changing from your usual together, happy self into a depressed person who worries endlessly about "his" life and problems. Oh, it will happen. I hope this note, letter, chapter, or section has given you some clues to find your own way in the jungle out there.

I used to read things like this and think, "What are these people telling me to do, join a convent?" I'm not. This is only meant to tell you that it's a nasty world out there, but you can make your own patch of it sane and safe. It's a tough job, but if enough of us do it, we can reach our dreams together more easily, and save lives in the process. Starting, obviously, with our own.

Epilogue

Fixing the Universe

We know we can't do the impossible. We know none of us can fix the universe, and we advise you to run like the dickens from anyone who tells you he or she has the magic solution to all the problems in your life or the world at large.

But we can end domestic violence in America, *one life at a time.* Together, we can change things.

We do not suggest that this will be an easy war to win. Many people make fun of the idea that we can end the violence. Even though it is a lofty goal, a near-impossible one, it is no more crazy than finding a cure for cancer. Do you know a single doctor or smart person who says there can never be a cure for cancer no matter how hard we try to find it? Domestic violence is no different. It is a problem we can work on, one case at a time.

Besides learning about the problem, which you have already done by reading this book, there are practical ways to help end violence. We hope that unless you are independently wealthy and have lots of free time, you will pick just one way to help. Otherwise, you will end up burned out. (It happens to many recovering victims.) Don't volunteer till you drop. Do a little bit, do it well, and know you have done your part.

The Number-One Idea: Write Letters
to Our Elected Officials

We would like you to become part of a massive grassroots campaign that will change politicians and policymakers. New laws and new attitudes in government are needed to provide for the needs of battered women. You are the key. If you will sit down and just write five letters—five handwritten letters—you can make a great difference. Letters sent to politicians translate in the recipients' minds into votes and money. This is an important principle that we all must understand. A politician sees each letter as a representation of a greater number of people who are thinking about this subject. They know that if one person actually writes them a letter, the subject is hot in that person's mind and in the minds of others. So please take the time to write these letters. This is how grassroots political reforms begin. When politicians get letters, they think money and votes.

Your letter should be *handwritten.* Either use this letter, which you can just copy word for word, or use the outline that follows it to compose your own letter:

Dear —————— :

I am writing to tell you that I've just finished reading the book Stop Domestic Violence *and that I am deeply concerned about this issue. Millions of Americans are affected by it, and I want to know what you are going to do about it. I am confident that you realize that many other people are interested in this issue but haven't written you. My friends and I are waiting to see what action you take.*

First, we want to see more shelters and more services for victims.
Second, we would like to see a national day care policy to help

women who have to leave violent relationships and start all over.

Third, what are you going to do to help treat men who batter women?

I know you have a lot to think about. I want to continue to support you in your office and future bids for reelection. I will be following your actions on this issue.

Sincerely yours,

Or you can compose your own letter, stressing at least these points:

1. You have just read this or another book (include the book's title) about domestic violence and are deeply concerned with what is happening in America.

2. You want to see changes made.

3. You want more shelters and more services for victims.

4. You want to be sure there is a national day care policy to help women leave violent relationships and lead full lives.

5. You want to see programs to work with batterers to help them out of their misery as well.

6. You want to see change and especially you want to know what this person is doing to change things.

Once these letters are written, get out your yellow pages or white pages and look up your U.S. senator and your member of the House of Representatives. (You can also call your local League of Women Voters for this information.) Fill in the names and write the names and addresses on plain envelopes. Sign the letters.

Now *do the same for your state legislature representative and senator* and your state's governor. For good measure, write one to the president; he's always in the mood to hear what America worries about. Tell him hi for all of the victims and survivors of abuse, and keep him interested in what we all care about.

Put the letters in the mail. You have spent one or two of the most productive hours of your life. If you do it, others will do it, and together we will have an impact on these politicians. We have to remember that in government it's the squeaky wheel that gets the grease. If we write them, changes will come.

Call some relatives and tell them what you did; ask them if they would do it, too, as a favor to you. Ask them to let you know when they've mailed the letters. Call a couple of friends and ask them to do it. Get friends in your church, your Bible study group, or any meeting you attend to do it as well.

The Number-Two Idea: Support a Nonprofit Organization Dedicated to This Issue

The Nicole Brown Simpson Charitable Foundation in California distributes money to shelters nationwide. You may want to donate to it and see the money go out and get spread around. You can also go out and donate to food drives and used-clothing drives and volunteer your time.

The Number-Three Idea: Doing Something Locally

Call your local YWCA and ask if they'll have a fund-raising drive for local shelters. Get a list of numbers. Join with friends to hold a garage sale to raise money, or just write a check for a small amount (or, if you have it, a large amount). Send it to a local shelter or to a local fund-raiser.

Give what you can of time and money. Volunteers make this country better every day. You'll learn the secret of volunteering: *you get back much more than you can ever give.* Volunteer work is a gift that never stops returning to you.

The Number-Four Idea: Help the System Get with It Locally

Go into your local police station and get brochures on domestic violence. If they don't have any, ask why not. Go to your local family court and ask the same questions. Go to law schools, emergency rooms, health clinics, and so on. Ask questions, be nice, find out what is being done. If nothing is being done, write some letters to the editors of your local paper.

The Number-Five Idea: Give This Book to a Friend

If you have done any of the above, or all of them, have a party. Celebrate. Give this copy of your book to a buddy, or tell them to read it. By learning about domestic violence and how to end it, you have saved the lives of people you don't even know. You deserve to hug yourself and celebrate the gift of life. You can come up with your own ideas and write to us care of the publisher so that we can improve new editions of this book with your own success stories. Thank you for caring enough about suffering people to read this book. You have helped in the healing by learning about the disease. You're an angel, and we love you.

Suggested Reading

The three books we recommend above all others are *The Batterer: A Psychological Profile*, by Donald G. Dutton with Susan K. Golant (Basic Books, 1995); *No Visible Wounds: Identifying Nonphysical Abuse of Women by Their Men*, by Mary Susan Miller (Contemporary Books, 1995); and *Next Time, She'll Be Dead: Battering and How to Stop It*, by Ann Jones (Beacon Press, 1994). Dutton testified on behalf of the prosecution as an expert witness in the O. J. Simpson trial; his book offers the best explanation of why these men do what they do and the type of therapy they can receive. The second book, by far the most heart-wrenching of the three, deals with the most widespread form of domestic violence. Ann Jones's book deserves all the wonderful endorsements it has already received. We suggest you read all three and also call your local bookstore and ask that they be stocked.

As practical handbooks, we recommend *The Battered Woman's Survival Guide: Breaking the Cycle,* by Jan Berliner Statman (Taylor Publishing, 1995), and *Domestic Violence Sourcebook,* by Dawn Bradley Berry (Lowell House, 1995).

A classic well worth reading is *Men Who Hate Women and the Women Who Love Them,* by Dr. Susan Forward (Bantam Books, 1987).

To help you with legal issues, get the *Divorce and Separation Legal Resource Kit,* by the NOW Legal Defense and Education Fund (available from NOW Legal Defense and Education Fund, 99 Hudson Street, New York, NY 10013), and contact the Association for Children for Enforcement of Support (ACES: 1-800-537-7072).

Two useful books for professionals are: *Domestic Violence and Children: Resolving Custody and Visitation Disputes: A National Judicial Curriculum,* by Nancy K. D. Lemon; and *Improving the Health Care Response to Domestic Violence: A Resource Manual for Health Care Providers,* by Carole Warshaw, M.D., and Anne Ganley. Both are published by the Family Violence Prevention Fund, 38 Rhode Island Street, Suite 304, San Francisco, CA 94103-5133. Phone: 415-252-8900; fax: 415-252-8991; e-mail: fund@igc.apc.org.

BOOKS ON DOMESTIC VIOLENCE

The following list was downloaded from the Internet. It is compiled by Susan Chalfin and Karen Michelle Mirko, and we offer it in the hope that domestic violence victims will get safe *first* and then begin their research on the subject. These books may offer a bit of help, advice, wisdom, and information, and may also have some really imperfect and wrongheaded advice for your situation.

Battered Wives
Del Martin
Volcano Press, 1976; revised and updated, 1981

A classic text, one of the first books to address domestic violence. Martin documents domestic violence in its entirety: the social constructs that enable men to abuse women, and women to stay; how legal services and social services can work against the victim; and how shelters work.

The Battered Woman
Lenore Walker
Harper & Row, 1979

Walker explains learned helplessness and the cycle of violence within the relationship. The book includes chapters on safe houses, legal and medical alternatives, and psychotherapy for women in abusive relationships.

The Battered Woman Syndrome
Lenore Walker
Springer Publications, 1984

An update of her previous book. Describes the psychosocial characteristics of battered women and their abusers. Contains chapters on the impact of violence in the home on children, the correlation of alcohol and drug use with violence, and psychological and legal responses to violent relationships.

The Burning Bed
Faith McNulty
Harcourt Brace Jovanovich, 1980

Based on the true story of Francine Hughes, who, after suffering years of abuse, burned her husband to death while he slept. Enlightens the reader as to how this woman could commit murder.

Called to Account: The Story of One Family's Struggle to Say No to Abuse
M'Liss Switzer and Katherine Hale
Seal Press 1984, 1987

A personal account by a Minnesota woman who after twenty years of abuse held her husband accountable and helped him change his violent behavior.

Chain Chain Change: For Black Women in Abusive Relationships
Evelyn C. White
Seal Press, 1995

An expanded edition of the first book on domestic violence specifically written for African American women.

Dating Violence: Young Women in Danger
Barrie Levy
Seal Press, 1991

Anthology including personal stories, essays by researchers and social analysts, intervention strategies, and education and prevention projects.

Domestic Tyranny: The Making of American Social Policy Against Family Violence from Colonial Times to the Present
Elizabeth Pleck
Oxford University Press, 1987

Documents the attention given to domestic violence from the first American laws against family violence in 1641 to the more recent, feminist-led, battered women's movement, and the forces that have shaped social reform.

Domestic Violence on Trial
Daniel Jay Sonkin, Ph.D., editor
Springer Publications, 1987

Contributions from authorities such as Del Martin, Lenore Walker, Anne Ganley, and Mary Anne Douglas examine the legal and psychological aspects of the battering syndrome. This is also available from Volcano Press (1-800-879-9636).

Every Eighteen Seconds: A Journey Through Domestic Violence
Nancy Kilgore
Volcano Press, 1992

In a series of letters to her son, Kilgore explains her relationship with her abusive husband. At the end of each letter are exercises to educate the reader and help her understand her own abusive relationship.

Feminist Perspectives on Wife Abuse
Kersti Yllo and Michele Bograd, editors
Sage Publications, 1988

An anthology of researchers and activists who present empirical data and narrative testimony on aspects of male violence against women from criminology to the Stockholm Syndrome.

Getting Free: You Can End Abuse and Take Back Your Life
Ginny NiCarthy
Seal Press, 1986

Comprehensive workbook for battered women. Delves into all aspects of intimate violence, from the social aspects of abuse, to self-help activities, to getting professional help, to restarting your life after you have left. Also has chapters on violence in lesbian relationships and between teenagers.

Healing Your Life: Recovery from Domestic Violence
Candace Hennekens
Pro Writing Services and Press, 1991

Written by a former battered woman, this self-help book examines the emotional aspects of being a battered woman and suggests steps to take to leave an abusive relationship. Also offers suggestions on how to build a healthy relationship.

Learning to Live Without Violence: A Handbook for Men
Daniel Jay Sonkin and Michael Durphy
Volcano Press, 1989

Workbook with exercises for men to help them manage anger constructively and change their behavior. Includes information on starting a self-help group.

Next Time, She'll Be Dead: Battering and How to Stop It
Ann Jones
Beacon Press, 1994

Analyzes the attitudes and institutions in society which contribute to domestic violence. Chapters deal with how the legal system leaves women unprotected, how language contributes to blaming the woman, and what can be done by different branches of society to eradicate the problem.

The Ones Who Got Away: Women Who Left Abusive Partners
Ginny NiCarthy
Seal Press, 1987

Thirty-three interviews with a diverse group of formerly battered women, who offer advice.

The Physicians Guide to Domestic Violence: How to Ask the Right Questions and Recognize Abuse
Patricia R. Salber, M.D. and Ellen Tallaferro, M.D. (cofounders of Physicians for a Violence-free Society)
Volcano Press, 1995

This is a how-to manual for doctors, caregivers, and medical trainees. Package is available for training groups.

Sourcebook for Working with Battered Women
Nancy Kilgore
Volcano Press, 1992

Written by a formerly battered woman who is now an educator on domestic violence, this manual offers suggestions for working with battered women and facilitating support groups, and provides the necessary supplemental material.

Trauma and Recovery
Judith Lewis Herman
Basic Books, 1992

Documents research findings on traumatized people, including combat veterans and victims of political terror as well as victims of sexual and domestic violence. Contains chapters on childhood trauma and the experience of chronic terror.

Violence Against Women: The Bloody Footprints
Pauline B. Bart and Eileen Geil Moran, editors
Sage Publications, 1993

A broad-based anthology that analyzes violence against women in the home, in the workplace, and in the streets. Covers types of violence, structural supports for violence, and the politics of institutional response to violence.

Violence Prevention: A Vision of Hope
Final Report of California Attorney General Daniel E. Lungren's Policy Council of Violence Prevention
Volcano Press, 1995

Ten common-ground initiatives designed to reduce society's "appetite" for violence. An authoritative source of information and ideas for advocates, lawyers, and lawmakers as well as anyone interested in reducing violence in America.

Violent No More: Helping Men End Domestic Abuse
Michael Paymar
Hunter House, 1993

Written by a training coordinator at the Duluth Domestic Abuse Intervention Project, this guide uses stories of both previously violent men and abused women, cultural explanations, and self-help exercises to help violent men change their behavior.

When Love Goes Wrong: What to Do When You Can't Do Anything Right
Ann Jones and Susan Schechter
HarperPerennial, 1992

Jones and Schechter, who have worked with women in abusive relationships, offer an analysis of "controlling partners" as well as concrete information on options women have in or out of the relationship, how they can find safety and support, and a list of resources.

When Battered Women Kill
Angela Browne
Free Press, 1987

Focuses on the patterns of violence in relationships involving the physical abuse of women by their male partners and the unfolding of events that lead to homicide committed by the woman victim. Also has chapters on the psychology of intimate relationships and the legal system.

When "I Love You" Turns Violent
Scott A. Johnson
New Horizon Press, 1993

In a clear and easy-to-understand style, this book provides definitions and examples of physical and emotional abuse. It describes the escalation and cycling of abuse and explains how abuse is learned. The emotional issues for the abuser and the victim are contrasted with the emotional environment of a healthy relationship.

Women and Male Violence: The Visions and Struggles of the Battered Women's Movement
Susan Schechter
South End Press, 1982

An activist and social service provider, Schechter documents the movement's history and growth. Offers feminist analysis of violence in the home and discusses the involvement of the judicial system and government in this social issue.

You Can Be Free: An Easy-to-Read Handbook for Abused Women
Ginny NiCarthy and Sue Davidson
Seal Press, 1989

Based on *Getting Free*, this simply written workbook for battered women covers all aspects of violence from defining the abuse to getting professional help from doctors, lawyers, and the police. Also has chapters on violence in lesbian relationships and between teenagers.

*Young Men's Work: Building Skills to Stop the Violence: A Ten Session
Group Program*
Paul Kivel and Alan Creighton
Hazelden, 1995

A multiformat curriculum written by the cofounders of the Oakland Men's Project. A complete package including handouts and video is available. This is also available from Volcano Press (1-800-879-9636).

BOOKS AND ARTICLES ABOUT GAY/LESBIAN DOMESTIC VIOLENCE

"Battered Husbands—Domestic Violence in Gay Relationships"
Michael Szymanski
Genre magazine, fall 1991

"Battered Lovers—The Hidden Problem of Gay Domestic Violence"
The Advocate, March 4, 1986

*Men Who Beat the Men Who Love Them: Battered Gay Men and
Domestic Violence*
David Island and Patrick Letellier
Harrington Park Press, 1991

Naming the Violence: Speaking Out About Lesbian Battering
Edited by Kerry Lobel for the National Coalition Against Domestic
Violence Lesbian Taskforce
Seal Press, 1986

Anthology of personal stories and the community-organizing strategies to support and empower battered lesbians.

"Not So Different, After All"
Patricia King
Newsweek, October 4, 1993

"The Scourge of Domestic Violence"
David Island and Patrick Letellier
Gaybook, winter 1990

"The Violence at Home"
Katrin Snow
The Advocate, June 4, 1992

Violent Betrayal: Partner Abuse in Lesbian Relationships
Claire Renzetti
Sage Publications, 1992

"When Gays Batter Their Partners"
David Tuller
San Francisco Chronicle, January 3, 1994

DATE AND MARITAL RAPE
National Clearinghouse on Marital and Date Rape
2325 Oak St.
Berkeley, CA 94708

The Clearinghouse offers an informational packet for ten dollars, and is an excellent resource for information about laws, books, and changing attitudes. They are responsible for making marital rape a crime in all fifty states.

License to Rape: Sexual Abuse of Wives
David Finkelhor and Kersti Yllo
Holt, Rinehart and Winston, 1985

A compassionate look at the experiences of women who were raped in marriage. Available through the National Clearinghouse on Marital and Date Rape for twenty-five dollars.

Rape in Marriage
Diana E. H. Russell
Indiana University Press, 1990

A study and resource guide on rape in marriage. Newly revised and expanded.

Wife Rape: Understanding the Responses of Survivors and Service Providers
Raquel Bergen
Sage Publications, 1996

An excellent resource.

DIVORCE INFORMATION
How to Avoid the Divorce from Hell
M. Sue Talia
Nexus Publishing Co.
2333 San Ramon Valley Blvd., Suite 150
San Ramon, CA 94583

We recommend this with one reservation: the book does not deal with domestic violence and is seemingly insensitive to many of the issues it creates. However, the book can help explain much of what happens in the process of divorce. Filter out anything that does not "click" with what you know about domestic violence, and use it only to explain the difficult process of divorce and custody.

EDUCATIONAL RESOURCES
Campus-Free College Degrees: Thorson's Guide to Accredited Distance Learning Degree Programs
Marcie Kisner Thorson
Thorson Guides
P.O. Box 470886
Tulsa, OK 74147
918-622-2811

This is an excellent resource for getting a college degree without spending a great deal of time and money. It covers high school degrees and is a tremendous resource for survivors looking to become financially more independent, fast.

RELIGION AND DOMESTIC VIOLENCE
Family Violence and Religion
David Charlsen et al., editors
Compiled by Volcano Press staff
Volcano Press, 1995

This book was designed to assist clergy and church workers of all faiths to counsel abused women, their children, and abusive men. Special emphasis is placed on diverse theology and cultures.
http://www.volcanopress.com
e-mail: Sales@volcanopress.com

The Shame Borne in Silence: Spouse Abuse in the Jewish Community
Abraham J. Twerski, M.D.
Mirkov Publications, 1996

This is an excellent sourcebook for people of all faiths. Twerski is a gifted writer and psychiatrist who founded Gateway Rehabilitaion Center, a not-for-profit drug and alcohol treatment center in western Pennsylvania, cited by *Forbes* magazine as one of the twelve best rehabilitation centers in America.

About the Authors

Lou Brown is president of the Nicole Brown Simpson Charitable Foundation.

- - - - - - - - - - - - - - - - - - -

François Dubau was pastor of Calvary Chapel in Laguna Beach. His ministry focuses on one-to-one counseling and the healing of damaged emotions and memories, which has led him to an understanding of the dynamics of domestic violence. He is a committed volunteer at the Nicole Brown Simpson Charitable Foundation and is developing a new ministry, *Arepagus*, designed to bring together people from different religions to forums dedicated to open discussions. In 1987 he co-authored a screenplay about AIDS, called *Colonies*, that was chosen for special recognition by the American Film Institute. - - - - - - - - - - - - - - - - - -

Merritt McKeon received her law degree from the Benjamin N. Cardozo School of Law in New York. A survivor of domestic violence, Ms. McKeon plans to work representing victims of domestic violence and hopes to improve the dismal state of legal education with respect to family violence by speaking, writing, and teaching. She currently teaches law at the American College of Law in Anaheim, California, writes briefs for attorneys in Orange County, and volunteers at the Nicole Brown Simpson Charitable Foundation. She lived in the Islamic Republic of Iran for seven years. During 1988 she lived in battered women's shelters in Portland, Oregon, with her three children.